baby BY THE NUMBERS

D1511155

baby

BY THE NUMBERS

A parent's quick reference
for essential
baby facts and figures

Richela Fabian Morgan
Foreword by Dr. Philippa Gordon
Illustrations by woolypear

CHRONICLE BOOKS
SAN FRANCISCO

Copyright © 2008 Quirk Packaging, Inc.

Library of Congress Cataloging-in-Publication Data available.

ISBN 978-0-8118-6594-4

Edited by Sharyn Rosart and Lindsay Herman

Design and Illustrations by woolypear

Typeset in News Gothic, Monticello, and Bryant

Manufactured in China

Chronicle Books endeavors to use environmentally responsible paper in its gift and stationery products.

10 9 8 7 6 5 4 3 2 1

Chronicle Books LLC
680 Second Street
San Francisco, CA 94107
www.chroniclebooks.com

Disclaimer

The ideas, procedures, and suggestions contained in this book are not intended as a substitute for consulting with your health care professional. Every baby is different and circumstances vary, so you should consult your own physician and use your own common sense. The author, publisher, and packager offer no warranties or guarantees, expressed or implied, in the completeness or advisability of the information contained in this book for your particular situation, and disclaim any liability arising from its use.

I would like to thank

Sharyn, (no last name needed), for her endless support and wisdom

Dr. Philippa Gordon,
for bestowing her wit and expertise on this project

The crew at Chronicle and Quirk Packaging

Lana Lê, one fabulous graphic designer

Dr. Brianne O'Connor and Dr. Edna Pytlak, my babies'
first pediatricians and extraordinary individuals in their own right

My loving husband, David

My endearing daughter, Masana

And Mack, my beautiful and exceptional son
You are my inspiration

And I dedicate this book to you.

CONTENTS

1

Growing Baby

Height, Weight, Skin, Hair, and Teeth

13

4

Interactive Baby

Language, Social, and Cognitive Development

63

5

Healthy Baby

Prevention and Common Ailments

81

FOREWORD

My father is fond of remarking, "Advice is the cheapest coin of the realm—everyone wants to give it away, and no one wants to take it." For new parents, the overabundance of advice begins early and lasts long. For example, a pregnant woman out for a short stroll may receive 3 to 5 varying opinions per block as to the sex of her baby. If she happens to be in a store or on a bus, others may chime in as well and a lively discussion can ensue, incorporating the folk wisdom and native medicine of many cultures. Should you find yourself in a situation like this, be sure to locate the exit, in case the discussion escalates and a scuffle breaks out. And, above all, do not reveal to the crowd that you've just come from the sonographer's office where you learned you are having twin boys. It will just disappoint everyone.

As your due date approaches, you will begin to consider the question of equipment for the baby. Here you will be aided by magazine articles such as "57 Must-Have Features of Your First Stroller" or "The Top 103 Strollers of the Year." Next, "66 Essential Items You Need to Have Before You Bring Your Baby Home." This one always puts me to shame because I've been practicing pediatrics for almost 20 years and my "must-have" list still has only 2 items on it (saltwater nose drops and a thermometer).

Advice from other parents on issues such as breastfeeding, circumcision, and vaccination may be accompanied by foaming at the mouth, so stand back. And, from your family, you can expect lots of help choosing a name—do remember that if you make a wrong move here, your extended family may still not be speaking to one another at your child's college graduation. Magazine articles on this topic can be useful—you will run across many such as "The Top 5 Celebrity Baby Names: Tobago, Kissinger, Anasazi, Virgin, and Buck." These will surely help you narrow your selection.

Once your baby is home, named, and appropriately equipped, new occasions for advice will arise. For the first 2 or 3 days, the baby will sleep all the time and refuse to feed, and for the next 2 days the baby will scream all the time and refuse to feed. If you are breastfeeding, one group of friends will tell you that you must supplement with formula, and the other group will assure you that the baby will never breastfeed if a drop of formula ever touches her lips. Another splinter group will opine that the baby would behave perfectly if you simply stop eating all the delicious foods that you have been avoiding for 9 months and were so looking forward to having. If you are bottle feeding, you will be advised by formula company literature to rush out and purchase

8

several other special formulas, and of course, there will be any number of advisors standing by to let you know you should be breastfeeding. Either way, you will be strenuously advised that your baby's normal and appropriate newborn behavior is your fault, because you didn't follow someone's advice.

Then the baby's face will erupt in hideous rashes just when the grandparents are due to visit, thus providing an opportunity, the first of many, for grandparental disapproval to undermine your self-confidence. Surprisingly, this is an area for potential advice that has not yet been well researched—I know of no book such as *What to Expect When You're Expecting Your In-laws*—however, no doubt this will soon be remedied and in the meantime you can probably pick up some hints on Web groups. Meanwhile you are on your own in the face of comments such as "None of you kids ever did that—are you sure it's normal?"

Having survived the initial period of self-doubt and grandparental kibitzing, and at last been rewarded with a social smile, the first really convincing evidence that your baby knows and likes you, you are ready to venture out into the world where new opportunities for received wisdom await you. For example, the first trip to the grocery store, where the baby will be pronounced overweight in aisle 1, underweight in aisle 2, cross-eyed in aisle 3, and inadequately clothed in the frozen food aisle. In new mothers' group, you will find that all the other babies are exclusively breastfed, sleeping through the night, achieving their milestones more rapidly, and that many of them are displaying strong evidence of being gifted and talented.

The explosion of books, Web sites, and chat groups for new parents provides endless opportunities to learn about everything you should be doing but aren't, and vice versa. The vehemence and conviction with which advice is offered is often unrelated to the actual expertise of the advisor. As an antidote to all that, this slim volume provides just the facts, and leaves space for you to learn about yourself and your baby your own way. The goal is for you to have information at your fingertips, and to enjoy the time you spend with your baby without worrying about doing things the right way. Simply by remaining calm and attentive, every parent can navigate the first year without elaborate programs, techniques, or philosophies. As I often remark to my patients, if it were that complicated, we'd be extinct.

—Dr. Philippa Gordon

JUST THE FACTS

This little book contains facts (that is, the straight dope and nothing extraneous, such as somebody's opinions) about infant and child care from birth to 3 years. That's it: a no-nonsense, straightforward, no-cutesy-time-wasting-stories book has finally arrived, and you (oh, lucky you!) are holding it in your hands.

Let's begin by examining a few of these facts:

FACT 1 this book can fit into a diaper bag without displacing any much-needed items such as wipes, an extra change of clothing, and, well, diapers, of course;

FACT 2 this book weighs approximately $1/8$ of most child-care guides, which makes it convenient to take it with you when traveling to far-flung reaches of the universe or the local coffee shop;

FACT 3 unlike your mother-in-law, this book does not tell you how to raise your child;

FACT 4 the format makes it easy to find the information you're looking for. See, having a baby isn't so scary!

Well-Baby Visits

Your baby, your circumstances, and your pediatrician will all dictate your particular doctor visit schedule, but this chart is based on generally accepted guidelines for well-baby pediatrician visits.

24 hours	2 or 3 days
Neonatal (within 24 hours of birth)	After birth/discharge from hospital

6 months	9 months	1 year	15 months

Look—you will end up with copies of all those other guides, those hefty tomes that cover everything you can possibly think of (and much that you cannot) with regard to infant development. You need these references to feel like you've done your due diligence, completed your research, and are ready to undertake what may be the hardest and most satisfying job of your life. And, heck, everyone has an opinion to share on how to do this or that. Breast or bottle? Cloth diapers or disposable? Diaper Genie or not? Many other parents will be all too happy to share their feelings on these weighty matters in as much detail as you can handle.

This book represents another way, a minimalist approach to parenting data: It has what you need—just the facts—in a nice, easy-to-use package. There's no need to sift through mounds of pages filled with well-meaning advice or scary-but-rare complications to get to the immunization chart or the baby-proofing list. Even better, you don't need instructions on how to use this book: Open it to the topic you're interested in, start reading. Done.

So use this book. And spend the rest of your time enjoying your baby's all-too-brief babyhood.

2 weeks	1 month	2 months	4 months

18 months	2 years	3 years	3+ years
			Once a year, every year, until age 21

Well-Baby Visit Checklist *First Year*

Know what to expect at each doctor visit and be sure to write down your questions so you don't forget. (Bring an extra diaper and be prepared to feed baby to offer comfort during vaccinations or in case of general dismay at being poked and prodded.) Here's a quick checklist of topics covered at a well-baby visit. Make a photocopy to bring with you and take notes.

- [ ] Height
- [ ] Weight
- [ ] Head circumference
- [ ] Cord care, circumcision (if relevant)
- [ ] Feeding schedule
- [ ] Peeing and pooping
- [ ] Sleeping
- [ ] Developmental milestones
- [ ] Eyesight, hearing
- [ ] Vaccinations
- [ ] Safety
- [ ] Specific issues (diaper rash, cradle cap, what's "going around," babysitting, etc.)

Your questions

....

....

....

....

12

Chapter 1

Growing Baby

Height, Weight, Skin,
Hair, and Teeth

Chapter 1   Growing Baby

GROWING BABY

New parents are a neurotic breed. Their list of things to worry about can seem as long as the Nile River and the number one thing to fret over is the normalcy of their child's growth. Get ready to spend a lot of time talking with a pediatrician. In fact, you might want to put her on speed dial. If you're still on the hunt for the right doctor, talk to people you trust—friends with children or other doctors—for references. Then, get to know the pediatricians themselves and find the best fit for you and your baby. See the Choosing a Pediatrician worksheet on page 113.

Height, Weight, and Head Circumference

During those well-visits with the pediatrician, the doctor will most likely throw around the word "normal" when weighing and measuring your baby. But "normal" turns out to be anything between the 10th and 90th percentile on the height, weight, and head circumference growth charts. Most pediatricians will tell you that what matters to them is a fairly consistent growth pattern. So a kid who starts out in the 30th percentile and stays more or less around that mark is a child with a healthy, consistent growth pattern—no worries. A baby whose numbers start out in the 90th then move steadily downward is cause for concern. Similarly, a child whose numbers zoom upward off the charts may also be at risk.

Oft-repeated but no less true is that every child grows differently. The genes of the parents play a huge part, so feel free to blame your own parents or those of your partner for the stature of your children.

On average, from birth to one year, a typical baby triples his or her birth weight and grows 10 inches (25 cm) in height. But not all babies do it at the same rate or in the same way—so don't worry about it: Ask your pediatrician—he or she gets paid to worry about these things.

Skin

Newborn skin is never perfect. It may be flaky, bumpy, pimply, or peeling. Rashes are common and may appear and disappear without any parental or medical interference. Never fear: Most of this is normal—if you're worried, show your pediatrician. Diaper rashes are very common within the first 15 months. You'll see tender patches of red, itchy, bumpy skin that can be very uncomfortable. Bad rashes might also cause pimples, blisters, and other sores—not incredibly pleasant for you or your baby. Prime suspects most often responsible for that pesky rash include too-tight diapers or clothing, lots of rubbing or wiping in the diaper area, long exposure to poop and urine inside the diaper, chemicals in soaps, baby wipes, detergents, or fabric softeners, new foods and their effects on your baby's poop output, and yeast infections, which can be caused by antibiotics. If the rash is accompanied by a fever of any kind, call your doctor immediately. (See Chart 5.4: When to Call the Doctor on page 86.)

Unless your newborn's skin is dry, baby lotions are not necessary. (So don't overbathe!) But if you do use one, choose an unscented baby lotion. Never use powder; dust and talc released into the air are not healthy for baby's lungs. After a few months, your baby may require more frequent moisturizing, especially during the colder seasons.

When you are out and about with baby, cover up and avoid direct sunlight. The sun's peak hours are from 10 a.m. to 3 p.m., so for a new baby opt for outdoor excursions in the early morning or the late afternoon. (Northern babies need to avoid sun only from May through October.) Put a hat on that vulnerable baby head. Once baby is 6 months old, use a water-resistant sunscreen with an SPF of at least 15 to 30 that provides broad spectrum UVA and UVB protection. At this point, you'll probably have to tie the hat on, so get one with straps. If you can convince your baby to wear sunglasses, be sure to choose a pair with certified UVA/UVB protection.

Hair

Anything goes. Some babies are born with a thick head of hair; some emerge pretty much bald. Some lose it after a few months, some don't. Some grow a luxurious thatch by their first birthday; others have to suffer the indignity of a baby comb-over until they're three. There is no magic potion to make a baby's hair grow, so you'll just have to wait.

Teeth

Teething usually begins around 6 months of age. However, your baby's first set of choppers can start coming in as early as 4 months or as late as 12 months. Symptoms of teething often begin a long time before an actual tooth breaks through the gums.

What to Expect from Your Newborn

It's true, your newborn is the most perfect little being to ever breathe air on this planet—who cares about a misshapen head, scaly or blotchy skin, and gooey eyes? All those post-delivery blemishes will vanish in time. Here's a list of common, nonharmful "imperfections" you might notice.

Head and Face

NEWBORN FEATURE	WHAT IT IS	DURATION
Soft spots	Fontanels, or spaces between your baby's skull bones	12 to 18 months for a front fontanel, and 6 months for a back fontanel
Elongated, oddly shaped head	Molding, caused by bones shifting during birth	Several days
Swollen spots	Caput, a swelling or bruise caused during birth	Several days
Crusty scalp	Cradle cap	6 to 12 months
Yellow gunk–filled eyes	Blocked tear ducts	Birth to 6 months
White spots on roof of mouth	Epstein's pearls, gingival cysts	3 months

Skin and Birthmarks

NEWBORN FEATURE	WHAT IT IS	DURATION
Fine hair on head, face, shoulders, back	Lanugo; baby body hair	1 month
Small, white bumps on the face	Milia, caused by blocked pores	1 to 2 months
Flaky skin	Shedding newborn skin	First few months
Baby acne	Yes, zits	1 to 2 months
Pink-and-blue marble-y skin when exposed to cold	Cutis marmorata	1 month
Splotchy red rash, with yellow or white bumps	Erythema toxicum	1 to 2 weeks
Flat pink or purple blotches on the eyelids, forehead, nose, and back of the neck	Stork bites, salmon patches, or the adorable "angel kisses"	1 to 2 years; stork bites on back of the neck may last longer
Raised red spots	Capillary hemangiomas, aka strawberries, temporary birthmarks	3 to 5 years
Bruise-colored spots on the bottom, back, or legs	Mongolian spots	3 to 5 years

Girls' Height *Birth to 36 Months*

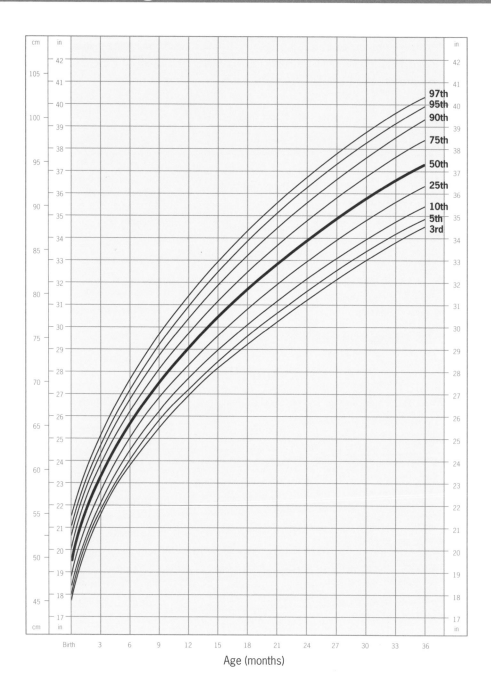

Age (months)

Source: Centers for Disease Control and Prevention, United States Department of Health and Human Services

Girls' Weight *Birth to 36 Months*

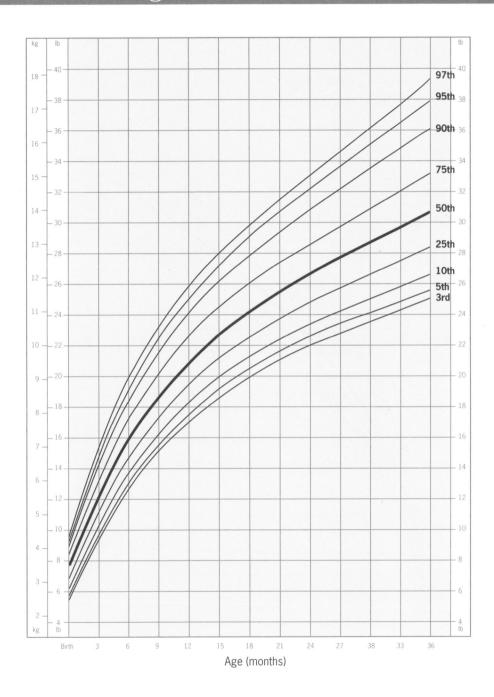

Age (months)

Boys' Height *Birth to 36 Months*

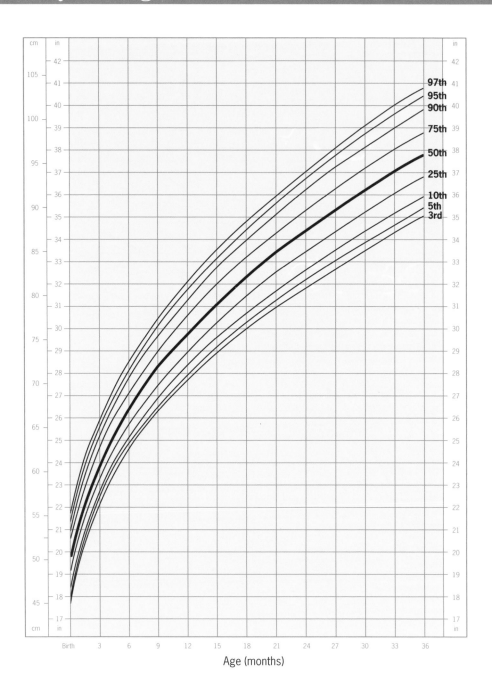

Age (months)

Boys' Weight *Birth to 36 Months*

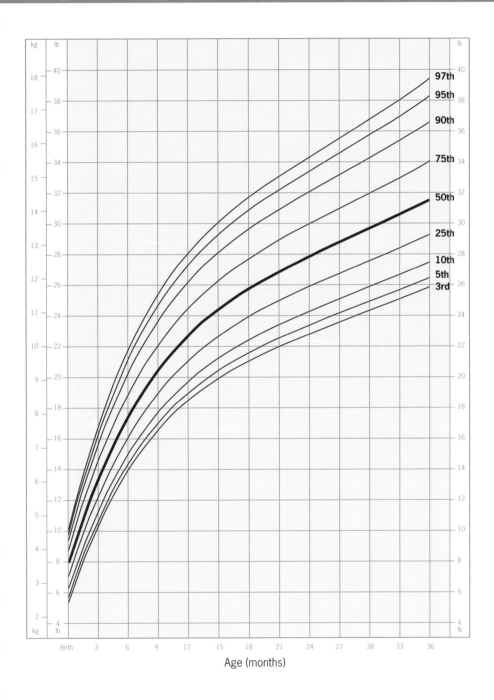

Girls' Head Circumference *Birth to 36 Months*

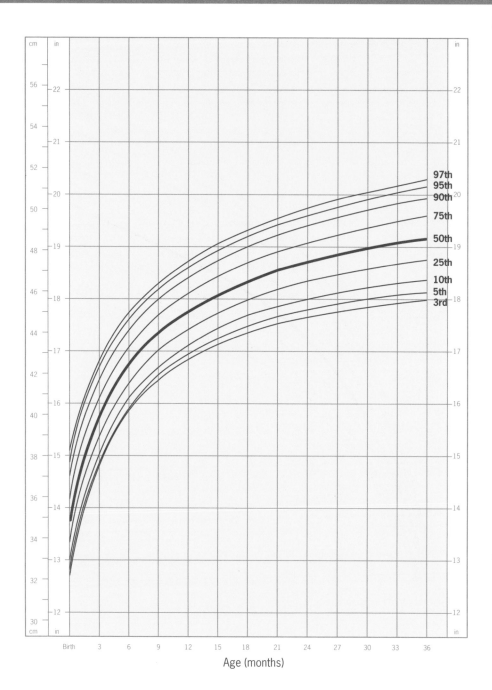

Boys' Head Circumference *Birth to 36 Months*

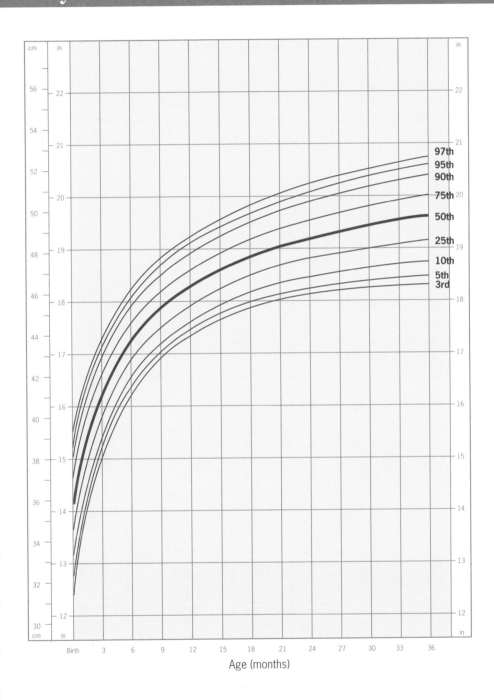

How to Bathe Your Baby

Give sponge baths until your baby's umbilical cord has fallen off and the circumcision wound (if any) has healed; after that immersion baths (i.e., in a tub) are fine. Use an infant tub with a nonslip surface at least until the baby can sit up unassisted. For the first few months of immersion baths, follow the steps for giving a sponge bath. After that, it's pretty easy and you'll know what to do. The room temperature should be around 75 degrees F (24 degrees C) and the bathing area should not be drafty; have the following supplies ready beforehand:

Soft washcloth
for soaping

Basin of warm water
(warm to the inside of
your wrist or elbow—
never your hand)

Soft washcloth
for rinsing

Towel to
cover the baby
during the
sponge bath

Cotton
balls

Gentle liquid
baby soap

Hooded towel
to wrap baby in after
the bath

Thick, soft
towels to lay
beneath the
baby

TIPS FOR TUB BATHING

- Never walk away or leave the baby unattended, not even for a second
- Do not overfill the tub with water
- Be sure to clean the tub after each use

Step-by-Step Newborn Bath

1 Place the baby on top of the towels; be sure to cover baby with a towel during the bath, uncovering parts as you clean them.

2 Using wet cotton balls, start cleaning at top of baby's face, moving from center of face to sides. Use a new cotton ball for each eye, moving from the bridge of the nose to the ear.

3 Wet the washcloth—do NOT add soap.

4 Gently wash the rest of the baby's face and head, being especially careful around the ears. Use a towel, not a cotton swab, to gently clean outside of the baby's ears.

5 Add a small amount of soap to the washcloth and wash the baby from the neck down, uncovering one area with the towel at a time. Use gentle and easy motions when washing the skin.

6 Wet the second washcloth and rinse soap off the baby's body, exposing one area at a time.

7 Wash the hair last. Use a small amount of baby soap on your first washcloth and gently wash your baby's head. Be especially careful of the fontenels.

8 Rinse the head by either using the second wet washcloth or gently pouring water over the baby's head. Be sure to not get water in the baby's eyes.

9 Place clean baby in a hooded towel.

Treating Dry Skin and Eczema

Even though babies are known to have the softest skin around, its sensitivity makes them more susceptible to dryness than adults. Mild dryness can be eased by keeping baths brief (under 10 minutes) and moisturizing (with a fragrance-free lotion) after every bath, especially during the winter months. If you notice dry, scaly patches of skin, make a visit to your doctor to see if your baby is developing eczema. Eczema is a very common skin condition experienced by many babies. Onset may be as early as 6 weeks, during baby's first winter, or upon introducing solid foods.

Guard your baby from dehydrating seasonal weather with protective winter clothes in the cold and sunscreen in the heat.

Limit your baby's bath to a maximum of 10 minutes.

Keep fingernails trimmed short so baby does not further irritate the skin by scratching.

Keep skin cool and try to prevent sweating.

Avoid wool, synthetic fabrics, and ill-fitting clothes that may rub and irritate the skin.

Do not use soap or detergents with perfume or other agents that will dry out or irritate the skin.

Liberally apply lubricants every day, whether or not the child is experiencing an exacerbation or remission.

Use thick lubricants: ointments (such as petroleum jelly) or creams. Avoid anything that contains mineral oil, alcohol, or a high level of water. Do not use lotions or oils.

Identify and avoid triggers. This includes food and environmental allergens.

Give frequent lukewarm baths. After bathing, apply lubricant within 3 minutes to trap moisture.

If your baby has eczema, give long baths that last about 15 to 20 minutes. Apply lubricants within 2 minutes after the bath.

Teething Symptoms

When a tooth is getting ready to break through, your baby may exhibit none, one, or several of the following symptoms:

- Increased fussiness

- Nighttime crying

- "Clingy" behavior

- Excessive dribbling (drooling)

- Chewing on fingers, teething rings, and other objects

- Swollen, red, inflamed gums

- Increased demand in breast or bottle-feeding (or just the opposite: rejection of breast or bottle because sucking hurts the gums)

- Poor appetite

- Interrupted sleep

Teething does NOT cause:

- High fever

- Diaper rash

- Diarrhea

- Lowered resistance to any infection

TIPS FOR SOOTHING TEETHING DISCOMFORT

- Gently massage the swollen gums with your finger (be sure to wash your hands thoroughly first).

- Give your child something cold to gnaw on, such as a Popsicle, a chilled teething ring (not a frozen one), or a frozen banana.

- Infant acetaminophen drops may be used for a few days if your baby is uncomfortable. Ibuprofen can be used, as well, and can be more effective than acetaminophen because it contains an anti-inflammatory component that acetaminophen does not. See the dosage chart on the box or on Chart 5.9: Acetaminophen on page 94.

Teeth Eruption Schedule

Primary Teeth

UPPER TEETH	ERUPT	SHED
Central incisor	8–12 months	6–7 years
Lateral incisor	9–13 months	7–8 years
Canine (cuspid)	16–22 months	10–12 years
First molar	13–19 months	9–11 years
Second molar	25–33 months	10–12 years

LOWER TEETH	ERUPT	SHED
Second molar	23–31 months	10–12 years
First molar	14–18 months	9–11 years
Canine (cuspid)	17–23 months	9–12 years
Lateral incisor	10–16 months	7–8 years
Central incisor	6–10 months	6–7 years

Tips for Healthy Teeth

- Do not allow the baby to nap or fall asleep with a bottle of milk or juice—the sugars will cause the tooth enamel to decay.

- Once the first tooth or teeth have begun to emerge, use a wet washcloth or sterile pad to wipe down the teeth and gums.

- Infant toothbrushes that slip over an adult's finger are also useful for massaging gums.

- When your child is ready for a toothbrush, choose one with soft bristles and a wide body (for a good grip). Do not use fluoride toothpaste until child is old enough to spit it out.

- Teach your child to brush after every meal, or at least twice daily.

- Visit the dentist before your child turns 3.

Basic Baby

Eating and Sleeping

Chapter 2   ## Basic Baby

BASIC BABY

Another feeding? Yup. Another dirty diaper? You bet. Your baby's needs are quite basic at first. They're also quite frequent. The good news is that there's not much guesswork involved: An infant's life mostly revolves around the principle of "what goes in must come out." The trick is figuring out how to make this routine work reasonably regularly, and understanding what to do if it does not. Many pediatricians will ask new parents to keep a record of what goes in and what comes out, and bring the record with them to appointments. When recording your infant's every pee and poo grows mind-numbing, remember that somewhere between now and the first day of kindergarten, your baby will eat more, sleep through the night, and learn to use the potty, during which process you will learn a thing or two about patience.

Feeding

According to the American Academy of Pediatrics, a baby should take in about $2\frac{1}{2}$ ounces (74 ml) of formula a day for every pound of body weight. For breastfed babies, it's harder to quantify since the amount baby receives can't easily be measured. Generally, newborns nurse every 1 to 3 hours—keep track of feeding frequency, and check with your pediatrician at the first visit. Your baby will let you know the number of feedings that will satisfy him on a daily basis, so let your baby call the shots (this is known among serious baby aficionados as "on-demand feeding"). There is no exact science to the nursing schedule and every baby is different. While a strict schedule may not work for you (known as "scheduled feeding," natch), you should know and stick to an approximate schedule of feedings per day.

Solid Food

Many experts say that babies should not receive anything but formula or breast milk until they reach 6 months of age. But if your 4-month-old is grabbing for the spoon, he may be ready for that first taste of rice cereal, while children who have food allergies in their family history may be on a slower track.

Remember that even as you begin feeding your child solid foods, she is still getting ALL her nutrients and calories from breast milk or formula. At 6 months, solid foods are introduced for taste and texture. The baby can take it, leave it, or throw it on the floor. And always remember that juices and water are NOT substitutes for breast milk or formula.

Some clues that your baby may be ready for solids (check with your pediatrician):

■ Your baby has doubled his or her birth weight.

■ Your baby shows an interest in the foods that you are eating and may try to grab the food from you.

■ Your baby consumes 32 ounces (946.1 ml) or more each day of breast milk or formula.

■ Your baby often puts things into her mouth.

■ Your baby can sit up with some support and can turn his head away when full.

Pee and Poop

In the beginning, it's a seemingly endless stream. Newborns should urinate a lot: about 8 times per day. And they also poop, but the frequency depends on their particular habits and whether they are bottle-fed or breast-fed. It could be once a day but it could also be once a week. Keep track (see Chart 2.5: In-and-Out Tracker on page 34), and talk to your pediatrician.

Potty training can begin when your child is between 18 months and 3 years of age. But there is no magical age by which it should be accomplished. Some parents are done with diapers when baby is a mere 18 months; others don't attempt to potty train children until they are between 3 and 4 years old. If your child can stay dry for at least 2 hours and has regular bowel movements, he may be ready. But even when you think that your child is potty-trained, accidents will happen—you might want to travel with an extra pair of underpants.

Nighttime dryness happens later, so do not expect a newly toilet-trained toddler to remain dry overnight. The hormone responsible for nighttime dryness, ADH, is typically produced in sufficient quantity sometime between 4 and 7 years of age.

Sleep

Babies sleep a lot! Parents do not. At first, babies wake frequently to feed. By about 3 or 4 months, depending on weight, eating habits, and temperament, most are ready to sleep a 4- to 6-hour stretch, which will seem like a miracle to you. If your baby has trained you well, you'll wake with a start, realize you've actually slept for 5 hours straight, and run frantically to the child to check that he is breathing. By the way, "sleeping through the night" really means 5 or more hours at a time. Bet you never considered that a full night's sleep before.

Newborns should always be put to sleep on their backs, never on their sides or stomachs. When baby learns to roll over, she may decide to sleep on her stomach. Do not keep running in and flipping her over like a flapjack; at this stage, she can determine her own sleeping position. (For more, see Chart 2.15: Safe Sleep Tips on page 52.)

Why Do Babies Cry All the Time?

Who knew that there would be such a symphony of crying: whimpers, moans, sniffles, tears, sobs, yells, screeches, and even shouts? Most babies have crying spells every single day—some last for 15 minutes, others for more than an hour. Some parents notice a regular fussy period, often in the early evening. Crying is an essential part of baby development and an infant's clearest form of communication before learning to talk. Uncovering the cause of baby anguish requires a bit of detective work, but in time, you'll be able to differentiate between a hunger cry, a sleepy whimper, and a poopy-diaper sob.

Top 10 Reasons Babies Cry

1 Dirty diaper

2 Hunger

3 Gas

4 Need cuddle time

5 Exhaustion from overstimulation

6 Illness

7 Boredom

8 Discomfort

9 General fussiness

10 Colic (chronic crying)

No-More-Tears Checklist

If your little one's feeling fussy, give the following tricks a try.

☐ Change diaper

☐ Burp

☐ Sing or talk

☐ Stroke back, arms, or head

☐ Set in a bouncy seat

☐ Pacify with a pacifier or a (clean) finger

☐ Rock baby in your arms, a rocking chair, or swing

☐ Adjust position or location for comfort (is it too bright or too loud?)

☐ Walk around with baby in your arms or in a stroller

☐ Feed

☐ Swaddle and cuddle

☐ Play soothing music

☐ Rub belly or back in case of gas pains

☐ Take a car ride

Is Your Baby Hungry? *How to Tell*

It's a very good idea to feed your infant before he gets hungry enough to start crying. For new parents who may feel mystified by baby's behavior, here are some common signs of hunger.

- Opening mouth

- Sticking out tongue

- Putting fingers and hands in mouth

- Cooing

- Moving head side-to-side

- Puckering lips

- Sucking on hands, clothes, blankets

- Snuggling into your shoulder or toward breast

- Fussing

- Crying (always try to feed before baby reaches a state of hard crying, as a hysterical infant may find it difficult to calm down sufficiently to feed)

Suggested Feeding Schedule
for the First Year

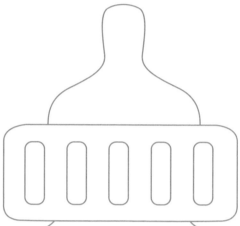

9–12 months
Breast Milk every 4 to 5 hours

Formula 24–31 oz (709.6–916.5 ml) / day

6–8 months
Breast Milk every 3 to 4 hours

Formula 24–37 oz (709.6–1093.9 ml) / day

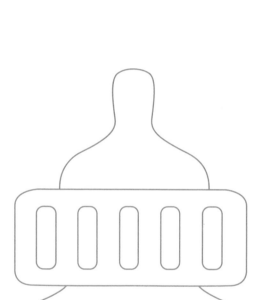

0–3 months
Breast Milk every 1 to 3 hours

Formula 18–40 oz (532.2–1182.6 ml) / day

4–5 months
Breast Milk every 2 to 4 hours

Formula 24–45 oz (709.6–1330.4 ml) / day

Breast Milk Storage Tips

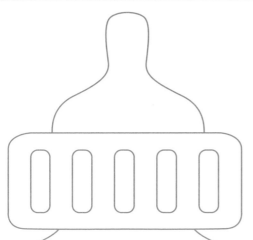

- Use a safe plastic bottle with a sealable top, or a sterile, sealable bag.

- Store your breast milk in amounts that you use every day to avoid wasting it.

- Store at room temperature (less than 77 degrees F or 25 degrees C) for 4 to 8 hours.

- Store at the back of a refrigerator for 3 to 8 days.

- Store at the back of a freezer for up to 3 months.

- Thawed breast milk can be refrigerated for up to 24 hours, but it should not be refrozen.

- When thawing the milk, do it slowly by swirling the storage container in warm water or by putting the container in the refrigerator the day before it is to be used.

- Breast milk can vary in color, and it is normal for breast milk to separate (the fatty part of the milk goes to the top). Shaking the bottle or sealed bag will mix the fat back into the milk.

- Don't use hot water to thaw breast milk.

- Never thaw frozen breast milk in a microwave oven. The milk could get too hot and burn your baby. Microwaving can also destroy valuable proteins in breast milk.

In-and-Out Tracker

Keep track of your little one's digestive system by recording her intake and output during the first week and beyond. Make copies of the worksheet below (or design your own version) so you can note the times of each feeding, pee, and poop to ensure all systems are running smoothly. This little composition will be your masterpiece of the infant period. Show your pediatrician. Long after you no longer need it, you'll get a kick out of seeing all the effort you expended tracking your offspring's poop.

week of ....

Day 1	FED									
	PEED									
	POOPED									
Day 2	FED									
	PEED									
	POOPED									
Day 3	FED									
	PEED									
	POOPED									
Day 4	FED									
	PEED									
	POOPED									
Day 5	FED									
	PEED									
	POOPED									
Day 6	FED									
	PEED									
	POOPED									
Day 7	FED									
	PEED									
	POOPED									

Diaper Changing Step-by-Step

Make sure all your supplies are nearby: clean diaper, wipes or wet cotton balls, diaper cream, waste bag or ridiculously expensive, complicated, yet still stinky diaper pail contraption. Keep one hand on baby at all times.

1 Spread out a changing pad or towel.

2 Lay your baby on his or her back and unfasten the diaper tabs or pins.

3 If there is a lot of poo, use the top half of the soiled diaper to wipe off the excess. Use wipes to thoroughly clean baby's skin.

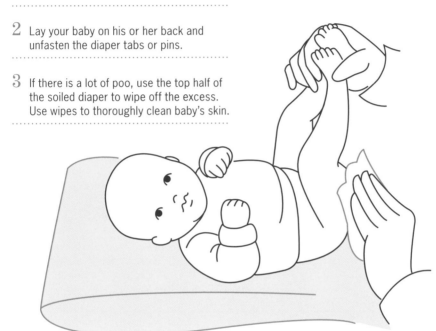

4 Raise the baby's butt by gently grabbing the ankles and pulling up. Slide out soiled diaper and roll into smallest possible hazardous-waste ball for disposal.

5 Slide clean diaper under baby and apply diaper ointment if needed, especially in the creases of the skin.

6 Fasten diaper tabs of the diaper and place dirty diaper in the waste receptacle.

7 Wash your hands after every diaper change.

FOR GIRLS

Using a baby wipe (or wet cotton balls for newborns), clean front to back to avoid getting any urine or fecal matter in the vagina.

FOR BOYS

Try to keep the penis pointed down and covered as much as possible to avoid getting a stream of pee in your eye, or up your sleeve.

Introducing Solid Food *When and What*

When your baby's ready for big-people food, start off slowly and mushily with a few soft grains and pureed fruits and vegetables. Then gradually introduce new foods as outlined in the schedule below. If you value your floor, put something down to protect it—something you can live with for about a year.

6 months

GRAINS

rice cereal
barley
oatmeal

FRUITS

apples (cooked)
bananas
pears (cooked)
avocado

VEGETABLES

sweet potatoes
acorn squash
butternut squash
green beans

7–8 months

FRUITS (all cooked)

apricots
peaches
prunes
mangos
nectarines
plums
pumpkin

VEGETABLES

carrots
peas
yellow squash
zucchini

PROTEIN

chicken
turkey
tofu

8–10 months

GRAINS

wheat grains
graham crackers
   (without honey)
multigrain crackers
multigrain toast
Cheerios (plain)
wheat germ

FRUITS

blueberries
cantaloupe
other melons
kiwi
papaya

VEGETABLES

parsnips
asparagus
broccoli
cauliflower
eggplant
white potatoes
onions
peppers
leeks
mushrooms

PROTEIN

egg yolks
beans/legumes
lean beef
pork
fresh ham (no
   preservatives)

DAIRY

plain yogurt
cream cheese
colby cheese
cottage cheese

10–12 months

GRAINS

pasta
wheat cereals
bagels

FRUITS

dates (quartered)
grapes (quartered)
cherries (pitted,
  quartered)

VEGETABLES

artichokes   spinach
beets   tomatoes
cucumbers

PROTEIN

white fish

DAIRY

cheddar
Gouda
Monterey Jack
Muenster
provolone

12+ months

FRUITS

citrus fruits
strawberries
all other berries

VEGETABLES

corn

PROTEIN

whole eggs

DAIRY

whole milk

12+ or 24+ months, if concerned about allergies

PROTEIN

shellfish*
tree nuts**
peanuts**
chocolate
honey

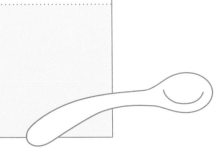

* Introduction of shellfish may vary, depending on family history of shellfish allergy.

** If there is a family history of a tree nut or peanut allergy, some pediatricians may recommend waiting until the child is 7 years of age.

Introducing Solid Food

Children with a Family History of Food Allergies

If there is a significant family history of food allergy (the child has a sibling or parent with an allergy), your baby may need to be on a slower food-introduction schedule. You should discuss the specifics with your pediatrician. For those with no such history, it is no longer recommended that foods be limited during the first year in hope of preventing the development of food allergies. To determine whether your child reacts to a food, closely monitor his reaction to each new solid food. Wait a few days before introducing the next new item.

6–9 months

GRAINS	PROTEIN
rice	lamb
millet	turkey

FRUITS (all cooked)	VEGETABLES (all cooked)
bananas	yams
pears	carrots
nectarines	potatoes
apricots	sweet potatoes
blueberries	beets
	all squash
	broccoli
	green beans
	cabbage

9–12 months

GRAINS	PROTEIN
barley	chicken
oats	veal
rye	beef

FRUITS (all cooked)	
apples	plums
prunes	pineapple
cranberries	raisins
grapes (quartered)	

VEGETABLES (all cooked)

asparagus
avocado
brussels sprouts
cauliflower

1–2 years

GRAINS	PROTEIN
corn	pork
wheat	fish
other grains	eggs
	ham (no preservatives)

FRUITS (all cooked)	DAIRY
citrus	cottage cheese
berries	yogurt

VEGETABLES (all cooked)

green peas
spinach
tomatoes
celery

Transitioning to Solids *Sample Schedule*

Common reactions to a first taste of "solid" food: Making weird faces, thrusting the food back out of the mouth, lunging for the spoon, smearing the food into the face and hair. Within a few weeks, it'll be clear what baby likes—and doesn't. Below is a sample schedule; the idea is to introduce new substances every few days and see how they go down, all while continuing your regular breast milk or formula feeding schedule. Substitute foods that work for you and your baby as needed.

⊶○ NEW

week 1	breakfast	lunch	dinner
MONDAY ⊶○	**rice cereal** (for the first serving, mix about **2 tbsp** (15 g) cereal with 1 oz (30 ml) breast milk or formula	rice cereal	rice cereal
TUESDAY	regular breast milk or formula feedings	regular breast milk or formula feedings	rice cereal
WEDNESDAY	regular breast milk or formula feedings	regular breast milk or formula feedings	rice cereal
THURSDAY	regular breast milk or formula feedings	regular breast milk ⊶○	rice cereal (if baby is tolerating cereal well, begin thickening mixture up to **4–6 tbsp** per feeding)
FRIDAY	regular breast milk or formula feedings	regular breast milk or formula feedings	rice cereal
SATURDAY	regular breast milk or formula feedings	regular breast milk or formula feedings	rice cereal
SUNDAY	regular breast milk or formula feedings	regular breast milk or formula feedings	rice cereal

Transitioning to Solids *Sample Schedule*

week 2	breakfast	lunch	dinner
MONDAY	rice cereal	regular breast milk or formula feedings	⚬ introduce another cereal (**oatmeal** or barley)
TUESDAY	oatmeal	regular breast milk or formula feedings	rice cereal
WEDNESDAY	rice cereal	regular breast milk or formula feedings	oatmeal
THURSDAY	oatmeal	regular breast milk or formula feedings	rice cereal
FRIDAY	⚬ **barley**	regular breast milk or formula feedings	oatmeal
SATURDAY	rice cereal	regular breast milk or formula feedings	barley
SUNDAY	⚬ oatmeal (mix cereals if you wish)	regular breast milk or formula feedings	rice cereal

week 3	breakfast	lunch	dinner
MONDAY	barley	regular breast milk or formula feedings	⊂○ introduce a puréed fruit, such as apples or **bananas**; if well tolerated, add a new fruit every other day
TUESDAY	oatmeal/bananas	regular breast milk or formula feedings	rice cereal
WEDNESDAY	⊂○ barley/**applesauce**	regular breast milk or formula feedings	⊂○ oatmeal/bananas
THURSDAY	⊂○ rice cereal/applesauce	regular breast milk or formula feedings	⊂○ barley/bananas
FRIDAY	⊂○ oatmeal/**peaches**	regular breast milk or formula feedings	⊂○ rice cereal/bananas
SATURDAY	barley/applesauce	regular breast milk or formula feedings	oatmeal/peaches
SUNDAY	rice cereal/bananas	regular breast milk or formula feedings	⊂○ barley/peaches

Transitioning to Solids *Sample Schedule*

week 4	breakfast	lunch	dinner
MONDAY	oatmeal/applesauce	rice cereal/**sweet potatoes** (add lunch; begin introducing vegetables)	barley/bananas
TUESDAY	rice cereal/peaches	sweet potatoes	oatmeal/applesauce
WEDNESDAY	barley/**pears**	bananas	rice cereal/sweet potatoes
THURSDAY	oatmeal/peaches	pears	barley/applesauce
FRIDAY	rice cereal/bananas	**peas**	oatmeal/peaches
SATURDAY	pears/applesauce	rice cereal	oatmeal/sweet potatoes
SUNDAY	barley/bananas	**carrots**	rice cereal/peas

week 5	breakfast	lunch	dinner
MONDAY	oatmeal/peaches	carrots/applesauce	barley/peas
TUESDAY	⊂⊃ bananas/sweet potatoes	⊂⊃ rice cereal/**green beans**	⊂⊃ oatmeal/pears
WEDNESDAY	⊂⊃ peaches/applesauce	⊂⊃ barley/sweet potatoes	⊂⊃ rice cereal/carrots
THURSDAY	⊂⊃ oatmeal/bananas	⊂⊃ green beans/**squash**	⊂⊃ barley/pears
FRIDAY	rice cereal/applesauce	peas/carrots	oatmeal/bananas
SATURDAY	⊂⊃ barley/**plums**	⊂⊃ sweet potatoes/pears	⊂⊃ rice cereal/green beans
SUNDAY	⊂⊃ bananas/peaches	⊂⊃ peas/squash	⊂⊃ oatmeal/plums

At first, your baby's foods should be almost watery, and then it can become chunkier in texture as your baby grows and is able to tolerate solids.

Common Allergies and Food Sensitivities

If your child is diagnosed with a food allergy, you must become a food-label detective. The Food and Drug Administration (FDA) requires manufacturers to list the eight most common allergens on food labels in plain language: cow's milk, soy, wheat, eggs, peanuts, tree nuts, and shellfish. These foods account for 90 percent of all allergies, so hone your food-label hawk eye to keep them and their many variations out of your child's mouth during the first year.

IF ALLERGIC TO

cow's milk

AVOID

milk: in all forms, from all mammals

casein and casein hydrosylates

caseinates

whey

lactalbumin, lactalbumin phosphate, lactogloulin, lactoferrin, and lactulose

butter: in all forms, including artificial butter flavor

buttermilk

cheese and cream cheese

cream, half & half, and ice cream

cottage cheese and curds

custard, pudding, and yogurt

ghee

sour cream, sour milk

IF ALLERGIC TO

eggs

AVOID

eggs: the entire egg, in all forms

dried egg, egg lecithin, lecithin (usually soy), egg powder, egg solids

albumin, ovalbumin, ovomucin, ovomucoid, ovovitellin, livetellin, globulin

fat substitute Simplesse (contains egg protein)

pudding, custard, ice cream, cake, cookies, meringues, cream- or fondant-filled chocolates, fudge, icings, and frostings

dougnuts, muffins, baking mixes

breaded meats or poultry

soufflé

egg noodles

egg drop soup

Hollandaise sauce

mayonnaise

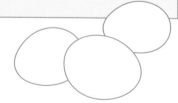

44

IF ALLERGIC TO
wheat
AVOID

wheat: in all forms

bulgur, durum, spelt, graham

kamut, semolina, seitan, triticale, couscous, and tabouleh

any product containing the word "gluten" (or a variation of this word)

dextrin

caramel color

extracts, including vanillin extract

breaded meats or poultry

praline and nougat

IF ALLERGIC TO
soy
AVOID

soy: in all forms

soy milk

soy beans (curd and granules), edamame

soy protein and hydrolyzed soy protein

soy nuts and soy sprouts

soy sauce, shoyu sauce, tamari

tofu and textured vegetable protein (TVP)

miso

natto

tempeh

IF ALLERGIC TO
peanuts
and tree nuts
AVOID

peanut butter and peanut oil; mixed nuts, arachnis oil

pesto; other crushed nuts in sauces

asian foods such as indian, thai, and chinese

hydrolyzed vegetable protein

marzipan; any candy with nuts

health food bars, energy bars, and sports bars

pastries with unknown ingredients, particularly carrot cake, pumpkin cake or pie

bouillon, Worcestershire sauce, gravy mixes

praline and nougat

muesli and fruited breakfast cereals

foods containing "nut essence"

vegetarian burgers, patties, loaves, and some casseroles

IF ALLERGIC TO
shellfish
AVOID

abalone

clams

cockle

conch

crab

crawfish and crayfish

lobster

mollusks, mussels

octopus, squid (calamari)

oysters

scallops

shrimp and prawns

snails, aka escargot

Swaddling Step-by-Step

for Newborns to 5 or 6 Weeks of Age

A snug, womb-simulating blanket wrap is one of the most effective calming techniques for babies (and even some adults). You'll get a rundown on the wrapping, or swaddling, technique while still in the hospital, but consult the instructions below for a handy refresher.

1 Find a blanket that is weather appropriate—warm for the winter, and light for the summer.

2 Lay it diagonally on a flat surface, so that it forms a diamond shape, and fold down the top corner toward the center.

3 Lay your baby on top of the blanket, with her head above the folded edge.

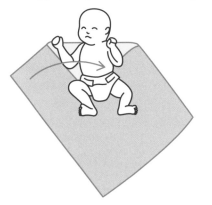 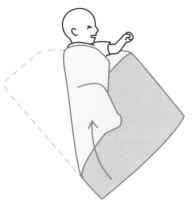

4 Keeping your baby's right arm against her side, wrap the right corner of the blanket around the width of her body. Tuck the corner under her left hip.

5 Hold the tucked-in corner against her left side, and adjust the blanket near her left shoulder to make the wrap taut.

6 Put your baby's left arm at her side, and fold up the bottom corner of the blanket. Tuck it firmly either into the V below her neck, or over her left shoulder.

7 Wrap the remaining left corner of the blanket over the front of your baby (or all the way around your baby, if the blanket is big enough), and tuck it into the V below her neck.

Sleep Needs *Birth to 36 Months*

Although it may seem that no one in your home is getting any sleep, your baby does get a fair amount of snooze—just not all at once.

AGE	AVERAGE TOTAL DAILY SLEEP (per 24-hour period)	SLEEP BREAKDOWN
0–3 months	**16 to 20** hours	Newborns should be awakened every 3 to 4 hours to eat until their weight gain has been established. Generally, they are only asleep 2 to 4 hours at a time.
3 months	**15** hours	10 hours at night (with an interruption), 5 hours during the day. Most babies are able to sleep through the night (5 or 6 hours) by 3 months of age.
6 months	**14** hours	10 hours at night, 4 during the day (2 naps). Most babies sleep through the night without a nighttime feeding.
1–3 years	**10 to 13** hours	Most babies are ready to eliminate the second daytime nap by 15 months of age. Toddlers may continue to take an afternoon nap until age 5, but many stop between 3 and 4.

Sleep Training Rundown

Warning to New Parents: Discussion of sleep training may elicit violent responses from other new parents whose views do not agree with yours. Be aware that the terms "Ferberize," "co-sleep," and "CIO" (that is, "cry it out") can all cause seemingly even-tempered people to become extremely agitated.

American Academy of Pediatrics

Encourage independent sleeping habits:

- establish naptime and nighttime routines
- set baby in crib before he's asleep, so he learns that cribtime is bedtime
- comfort crying baby in crib, but do not take him out
- let baby cry in crib for a few minutes to give him time to fall asleep on his own

FURTHER READING

American Academy of Pediatrics Guide to Your Child's Sleep by George J. Cohen, MD, FAAP

Ferber Method (aka "Cry It Out")

Encourage self-soothing independent sleeping habits:

- establish naptime and nighttime routines
- teach baby the difference between daytime and sleeptime
- place baby's crib in a separate room from your own
- visit crying baby after regular and progressively longer intervals, but do not take him out
- rub baby's belly or sing to soothe him

FURTHER READING

Solve Your Child's Sleep Problems by Richard Ferber, MD

Karp Method

Recreate womb-like environment:

- swaddle
- swing
- say "ssshhhhh"
- let baby suck on pacifier

FURTHER READING

The Happiest Baby on the Block: The New Way to Calm Crying and *Help Your Newborn Baby Sleep Longer* by Harvey Karp, MD

48

However, you will find many books on the various methods, and you can do your research behind brown paper covers. Here's a quick rundown of the most popular sleep training philosophies. Find what works for you and don't worry about what other people think.

Sears Method (aka Attachment Parenting)

Implement parent-child calming-down routines to ease baby to sleep:

- close sleeping
- co-sleeping
- cuddling
- sling-carrying
- massaging

FURTHER READING

Nighttime Parenting: How to Get Your Baby and Child to Sleep by William Sears, MD

Weissbluth Method

Respond to your baby's natural sleep cycles to make sure he sleeps when tired:

- look for signs of drowsiness and encourage regular naptimes
- turn down lights and sounds during naptime and nighttime
- calm baby when crying
- do not rush to crib when baby cries

FURTHER READING

Healthy Sleep Habits, Happy Child: A Step-by-Step Program for a Good Night's Sleep by Marc Weissbluth, MD

No-Cry Method

Create a flexible sleeptime and daytime schedule:

- maintain a sleep log of your baby's habits
- establish a naptime and nighttime routine
- distinguish daytime naps from nighttime sleep by setting baby down for a nap in a lit room and only changing into pajamas at night
- soothe crying baby

FURTHER READING

The No-Cry Sleep Solution: Gentle Ways to Help Your Baby Sleep Through the Night by Elizabeth Pantley

Fill-in Sleep Chart

Keeping track of baby's sleep—including naps—will help you begin to create a daily schedule that works for your family. The chart below covers one week's worth of sleep, so make copies and keep them handy. Color in each hour or part hour that baby is asleep. Over the course of the week, you should see

		S	M	T
AM	7			
	8			
	9			
	10			
	11			
PM	12			
	1			
	2			
	3			
	4			
	5			
	6			
	7			
	8			
	9			
	10			
	11			
AM	12			
	1			
	2			
	3			
	4			
	5			
	6			

some patterns emerging—naps at approximately the same times and fairly consistent nighttime sleep patterns. Plan baby's day accordingly, and you both will get some good rest!

W	T	F	S

Safe Sleep Tips *for Infants*

Make sure your infant is sleeping safely by taking the following measures, which may significantly reduce the risk of Sudden Infant Death Syndrome (SIDS). The exact causes of SIDS remain unknown, but risk factors include stomach- and side-sleeping; soft bedding or toys in the sleeping area; a too-soft mattress; cigarette smoke; and overheating. The slogan "Back to Sleep" will help you to remember the most important rule.

- ALWAYS position your baby on his back for sleep—whether at night or at naptime.

- Let your baby play on his stomach, but NEVER let him sleep on his stomach.

- Do not use any type of loose bedding, such as blankets or quilts, in baby's crib. There should be nothing in baby's bed except baby.

- Outfit your baby in infant-sleeper clothing appropriate to the climate. He should be comfortable without needing a cover.

- Ensure that baby's room is at a cool, comfortable temperature—baby's room should not be overheated.

- Put baby to sleep on a proper baby mattress that is firm, not soft. Do not use a waterbed.

- Crib sheets should be snugly fitted to the mattress.

- Do not surround a sleeping baby by pillows, quilts or blankets, or soft toys.

- Never place pillows in baby's crib or sleeping area.

- Keep tobacco smoke away from baby.

- Make sure clothing has no loose strings or ties.

- Offer baby a pacifier—pacifier use has been associated with lowered risk.

- Many experts recommend sleeping nearby (i.e., in the same room) but not in the same bed with your infant, though there is much debate on this topic. Never sleep with your baby on a couch, sofa, or lounge chair.

- Breast-feed if possible; breast-fed babies have a lower incidence of SIDS.

- If your baby ever has periods of not breathing, turning blue, or going limp, tell your pediatrician immediately.

- Avoid exposure to respiratory or gastrointestinal infections.

- Be sure all caregivers are aware of these recommendations.

Active Baby

Physical Development

Chapter 3   Active Baby

ACTIVE BABY

Panicky parents: Listen up. There's no magical "deadline" for development milestones—on the contrary, part of the magic is watching your baby learn and grow at her own pace. Yours may be quick to achieve some physical milestones and seem like she'll never reach others. Some babies walk at 9 months, while others wait until 18 months before deciding to get on their feet. Try not to compare your baby's physical development to other children's, and don't panic if junior's main form of locomotion at 13 months is a backward crab crawl. If you sense your child is lagging in more than one developmental area, talk to your pediatrician.

Kick Start Your Baby's Development

Although they can't talk, walk, or shoot hoops just yet, newborns do have innate skills, strong senses, and their own modes of communication. Even at birth, healthy babies can see human faces within a 12-inch distance—or the distance from a mom's chest to her eyes. Those first loving, fascinated gazes at mom and dad are the earliest moments of parent-child bonding. Newborn senses help them learn and develop more advanced social skills—whether they're hearing the soft melody of a musicbox, watching a mobile above a crib, or using their sense of smell to find a mother's nipple. As your newborn gets older, you'll see these skills sharpen and multiply in no time.

While knitting or catching fly balls with baby is not in your immediate future, you can play with your baby in a way that encourages her growing sensory awareness and physical development. Massages help stimulate your baby's brain, muscles, and motor skills, while also regulating the respiratory and digestive systems, relaxing the nerves, and easing any pain caused by teething. Also, be sure to pick up your baby and dance around, play with her hands and feet, pour water over her hands, tickle her tummy—all this activity will get her baby mojo flowing and encourage her development.

Baby's Got Skills! Motor Skills, That Is

Gross motor skills refer to the control of the big muscles in the body: lifting the head, rolling over, sitting, crawling, standing, cruising, and walking. A baby develops these skills starting from the top of the body and gradually working the way down to the bottom. Expect to see her first show control of her head and neck, then her shoulders, arms, hands, upper torso, hips, pelvis, and, finally, her legs. Your baby will go from bobble-head to romper in roughly a year, one of the busiest years of her life.

Fine motor skills refer to the precise coordination of the smaller muscles, like the fingers, toes, lips, and tongue. A classic example of a fine motor skill is the baby's ability to grab objects with her hands or visually track an object as it moves around the environment. You'll see your baby first learn to grasp with her fist and tiny fingers, then control her entire arm, and then the individual parts of her arm from her elbows to her fingers. Within the second year, your baby will start developing hand-eye coordination and hand-hand coordination.

Practice and repetition is crucial in helping kids refine their motor skills—to strengthen both their muscles and their brain development. Be aware of the motor milestones for each age range so you can keep your baby busy with the right activities for an optimal and well-rounded workout. And remember that what seems like all fun-and-baby-games will actually go a long way in stimulating your child's growth.

How to Massage a Baby

Massage has been shown to improve baby's digestion; encourage longer, deeper sleep; lessen crying; and even improve mood—for both baby and massager. Try these relaxing strokes. Then book a massage for yourself.

BEFORE YOU START

Use massage oil; be sure to choose one that is light, organic, and cold-pressed from a vegetable source, such as apricot kernel or grapeseed. Do not use lotions, nut-based oils, or nonorganic/nonfood petroleum-based oils. If your baby has a fever, has just had an immunization, or is ill, wait for another time.

Basic Technique

Pour massage oil on your hands. Never pour anything directly on baby.

Hand pressure should be comfortable but stimulating—about the same pressure you would use on your eyelids without causing any discomfort.

On small areas of your baby's body, use your fingertips; on larger areas like his back, use the palms of your hands.

As a general rule, strokes should be soft, long, slow, and rhythmic, moving from the center of your baby's body outward.

Keep your movements balanced; if you massage the left arm, also do the right arm.

With newborns, avoid the umbilical cord area and circumcision site (if your baby has been circumcised).

Start with a short session at first, no more than about 5 minutes. Over time, you can lengthen your massage sessions to 20 minutes, basing the length of time on your baby's signals of enjoyment.

STROKE 1

Arm and Leg Swoops

With baby on his back or in your lap, facing outward, wrap fingers and palms around baby's arm or leg to form a "C" shape that molds to the flesh of his leg. Place one hand at the top of baby's thigh, and the other just below it.

Glide the bottom hand, followed by the other, the full length of baby's leg from top to ankle. For arms, move from shoulder to wrist.

STROKE 2

Chest Swirls

With baby on his back, place your palms flat in the center of baby's chest, fingertips resting just above the bottom of his ribcage.

Slide both hands together up toward baby's chin, then outward and downward in a circular motion, hands meeting back at their starting position.

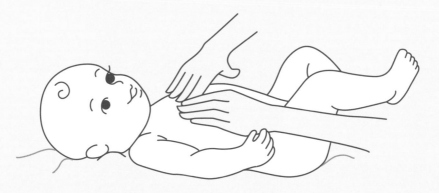

Tummy Touches

Lay your baby on his back and, with one hand, place the tips of your index and middle fingers on his tummy—midway beneath his chest and his belly button.

Gently slide your fingers one at a time across the width of his tummy, and then repeat in the opposite direction. Apply enough pressure to make a slight impression into your baby's skin.

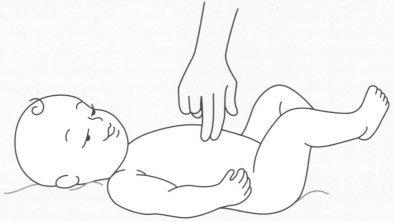

Cheek Swirls

Lay your baby on his back, or sit him up so he faces you.

With the tips of your index and middle fingers, rub circles in your baby's cheeks, occasionally changing directions.

Motor Milestones *for the First Year*

A milestone is just a word, right? Right . . . The sensible side of you knows each one is simply an approximation. Yet you become rabid over these milestones and watch your baby like a hawk as he does . . . well, mostly nothing. Then a miracle: baby raises his head for the first time. Immediately, birds start singing, the sun shines through parted clouds, and life is euphoric—until you start fixating on what should happen *next* month.

APPROXIMATE AGE	GROSS MOTOR SKILLS	FINE MOTOR SKILLS
1 month	briefly lifts head up	makes a tight fist and will hold an object firmly when placed in hand
2 months	can hold head at a 45-degree angle from a flat surface	gains better control of hands and grasps
3 months	lifts and holds head up at a 90-degree angle from a flat surface	opens palm weakly with little strength to grasp objects
3–6 months	uses hands to support self while sitting rolls from back to tummy can support weight with legs while standing	reaches for toys but may not get a firm grasp reaches both hands to play with feet sucks on hands visually tracks a moving object
6–9 months	sits and reaches for toys without falling down moves from tummy or back into sitting position attempts crawling	transfers an object from one hand to another finger-thumb grip develops, and can examine an object using both hands hands are relaxed and open most of the time
9–12 months	pulls to stand and cruises along furniture stands alone and takes several independent steps before falling down	finger-feeds self releases an object from grip at will uses thumb and pointer finger to pick up tiny objects (pincer grasp)

Play-and-Grow Activities *for the First Year*

To help your baby reach those aforementioned milestones, try the following activities to get him moving.

0–3 months

STIMULATE THE SENSES

Funny faces: Stick out your tongue and wiggle it around. Wrinkle your nose—babies love faces.

Tummy time: Either using an activity blanket or lying with your baby on a rug, move brightly colored objects toward the baby.

Mobile: Place one above the crib or changing table, and be sure it's well out of your baby's grasp.

Unbreakable mirror: Your baby will be fascinated by his own face.

Cuddle me: You should be an expert cuddler by now.

3–6 months

DISCOVER THE BODY

"Gotcha": Pretend to "catch" your baby, and stimulate him with gentle tickles.

Up and away: Lift the baby high in the air (don't throw him yet, and NEVER shake).

Squirt me: Gently pour and squirt water on your baby in the bathtub.

Piggies: "This Little Piggy" is the old standard, but any rhyme or song you like will do. Try other body parts, too.

Tasty: By 6 months, your baby will be placing everything from his fingers to yours into his mouth. So collect nontoxic, safe items for him to explore this way.

Toys to get: Rattles, play gyms, squeaky rubber toys, cloth books, teething rings.

6–9 months

GRABBING AND GRASPING

Household objects: Anything is a toy at this age, from wooden spoons to plastic food containers with lids.

Droppables: Baby drops it, you pick it up (bend from the knees, please). Be ready to repeat—often.

Please and thank you: Hand him a toy, ask for it back; repeat.

Reach out: Place a toy just out of baby's reach on the floor or rug; encourage him to get it.

Toys to get: Plush toys, cribside activity board, balls, soft building blocks, board books, bubbles.

9–12 months

IN MOTION

Fill and dump: Anything is fair game, whether it's water, sand, or toys. Expect your baby to do this over and over . . . and over again.

Pile up: He'll love stacking blocks, cups, what-have-you . . . only to knock them over and start again.

Catch-me: "Chase" your baby to encourage movement.

Edible toys: Kids love playing with their food, so give your baby cooked green peas or cereal Os and let him go at it. Watch in amazement as the pincer grasp is deployed.

Toys to get: Balls, shape sorters, push toys, toy phone, board books, building blocks, stacking boxes.

Motor Milestones *for Toddlers*

It'll be a while before those flailing little hands can actually close on a ball and throw it to first base or those chubby little legs can perform a plié, but it'll happen eventually. In the meantime, baby will go from wobbly first steps to running fast enough that you have to put on some speed to keep up. Here's a preview.

12–18 months

GROSS MOTOR SKILLS

stands alone for 10 seconds or longer

walks without help

stoops and stands back up independently

bends over and looks through her legs

walks backward and sideways, and begins to run

pushes, pulls, or carries a large toy while walking

starts to climb into a small chair independently

climbs up stairs with support, placing both feet on each step

FINE MOTOR SKILLS

puts a few too many objects into a container before taking them out

marks a piece of paper with a crayon and scribbles imitatively

stacks 2 or 3 blocks

turns more than 1 page at a time in a board book

can hold an object with 1 hand and manipulate it with the other hand

18–24 months

GROSS MOTOR SKILLS	FINE MOTOR SKILLS
walks down stairs with support, placing both feet on each step	imitates drawing a vertical line
jumps in place	manipulates an object with fingers and thumb alone
sits directly in a small chair	turns pages of book one by one
runs the length of a room without falling down	zips and unzips a large zipper
stands on 1 foot momentarily	attempts to put on shoes
picks up toy from floor when standing up	attempts to put familiar objects away
	unwraps wrapped foods like crackers

24–36 months

GROSS MOTOR SKILLS	FINE MOTOR SKILLS
runs forward well	strings 4 large beads
jumps in place, 2 feet together	turns single pages
stands on 1 foot with aid	snips with child-safe scissors
walks on tiptoes	holds crayon with thumb and fingers, not fist
kicks ball forward	uses 1 hand consistently in most activities
	imitates circular, vertical, and horizontal strokes
	paints with some wrist actions, makes dots, lines, and circular strokes
	rolls, pounds, squeezes, and pulls clay
	removes all clothes without help

Play-and-Grow Activities *for Toddlers*

12–18 months

MASTERING THE BIG MUSCLES

Walking up and down stairs: Better than a Stairmaster!

Pushing and pulling a cart or baby stroller: She's learning to control her own strength.

Dancing: It's not quite Fred Astaire, but it'll bring a smile to everyone's face.

Sand toys: She'll love digging, combing, making forts and castles—and then destroying everything!

18–24 months

GETTING THE RIGHT TOUCH

Dress up: Let her button and unbutton a shirt, undo a clasp, and tie a shoe (or at least attempt to).

Toy piano, xylophone, and other musical instruments: This will be a great way to inspire any musical inclinations, when she's not pounding the heck out of the instrument.

Rocker: Too much force will make her fly out of her seat, but just the right amount will give her endless pleasure.

2–3 years

FINE TUNING THE HAND-EYE (AND HAND-FOOT) COORDINATION

Stringing beads: It's harder than it looks, but very satisfying if a child can do it.

Tricycle or "Big Wheel": The precursor to the two-wheeler and training wheels.

T–ball set, soccer, and kick balls: Any of these will help develop body coordination, and encourage running. Look out, David Beckham!

Simon Says: Jumping on one foot while rubbing your tummy AND patting your head—now that's exercise!

Toddler-safe swing set: Just be sure it's low to the ground just in case she loses her balance.

Interactive Baby

Language, Social, and Cognitive Development

Chapter 4   **Interactive Baby**

INTERACTIVE BABY

Believe it or not, a newborn's brain weighs approximately $\frac{1}{4}$ of what an adult brain weighs, but by age 5 has reached almost its full weight. This is NOT to say that by age 5 your child should be able to think and reason like an adult (although I'm sure you know some adults who are about as reasonable as a 5-year-old). Progress is fast, from gleeful gurgles to eloquent pleas to strict orders on what they want . . . NOW.

Your tiny, helpless infant will soon learn to push buttons (literally and figuratively). In addition to her physical development, your baby is going to acquire a bunch of other skills. Here are the main categories:

SPEECH AND LANGUAGE—the child's ability to both understand and use language

SOCIAL AND EMOTIONAL—the child's ability to interact with others, including helping themselves and learning self-control

COGNITIVE—the child's ability to learn and solve problems

You can help

Fortunately, most kids will learn this stuff whether you help them or not—but since you went to all this trouble already, why not give the kid some assistance? A stimulating, loving environment goes a long way toward ensuring that your baby develops appropriately in all ways. The PlaySmart Activities listed in this chapter are a good start. Even if it seems like your baby is not aware of what the heck is going on, she is actually soaking up a huge amount of information.

Studies show that being plopped in front of a television screen, even one showing a program supposedly designed to give your baby the brainpower of (insert name of famous physicist here) does nothing, i.e., not one thing, to stimulate a baby's intellectual growth. Some researchers even suggest shunning television completely until age 2. That said, it can be hard to avoid, and a little TV-watching is unlikely to have much effect on junior's IQ in either direction. However, you might like to try some learning-intensive toys and activities instead. Keep playing with her and watch as, almost without warning, she changes from indifferent observer to enthusiastic participant.

Speech and Language Development
Milestones *for the First Year*

0–3 months

has different cries for different needs

coos or vocalizes other than crying

quiets or smiles in response to sound or voice

turns head toward direction of sound

3–6 months

begins to use consonant sounds in babbling, e.g., "dada"

uses babbling to get attention

6–9 months

increases variety of sounds and syllable combinations in babbling

imitates others in simple play

looks at familiar objects and people when named

9–12 months

meaningfully uses "mama" or "dada"

produces long strings of gibberish (jargoning) in social communication

responds to simple commands, e.g., "come here"

may turn head when called by name

Speech and Language PlaySmart Activities *for the First Year*

Babies learn language by hearing it and imitating what they hear. The best way to help your little babbler acquire language skills is to talk with him—all the time. At first, you'll have to take both parts of the conversation (give him space to "answer") but it won't be long till he's talking your ear off.

Talk the talk

Speak slowly and clearly to your baby. Don't use "baby talk," but do speak emphatically.

Use short sentences, which will give him a chance to hear distinct key words instead of a confusing jumble.

Figure out what your babbling baby is trying to say and show that you see the connection between the babble and the object or person he's babbling about. For example, "dadada" is most likely referring to his dad, and "baba" might be his bottle.

Walk the walk

When you talk to your baby, point out the objects and people as you say their names.

Be animated and make eye contact to engage your baby. He'll see how your mouth moves when you talk.

Show an interest in what your baby has to say, even though it's in gibberish.

Play it again, baby

Sing repetitive rhymes and kids' songs to your baby. He will grow familiar with the sounds and cadences.

Exaggerate and repeat key words to turn this vocab-building into a game. The all-too-familiar "gotcha nose" game is familiar for a reason.

Read, read, read

It is never too early to read to a baby. Read as often as possible.

Ask questions about the pictures in the books so that your baby is interacting with you. (Although you may have to answer your own questions, at first.)

Speech and Development Milestones

for the Second Year

12–15 months

vocabulary consists of about 5 words

understands 50 words

waves

imitates new less-familiar words

points to and reaches for objects

15–18 months

can speak about 10 words clearly

may refer to self by name

uses a combination of simple words, inflection, and body language to get point across

18–24 months

may link 2 or 3 words together to form a sentence

identifies parts of own body

tries to hum or sing

points to pictures in a book upon request

listens to nursery rhymes and short songs with fingerplay

imitates sounds, words, or body movements

may be able to use the words "please" and "thank you" if prompted

Speech and Language PlaySmart
Activities *for the Second Year*

The more time you spend communicating with your baby, the better.
Engaging her in conversations—even if most of her words are still
unintelligible—will go a long way to building her vocabulary.

Get your baby started

Ask questions, especially ones that she already knows the answer to.

Give your child time to respond. Don't rush, although you may have to answer your own
questions at first.

Speak when spoken to

Try to interpret what your child is saying and respond to her, even if you have no idea what
she's babbling about.

Talk in an upbeat, excited way to keep your baby engaged.

Give the play-by-play

Narrate your baby's actions. If she's reaching for a teddy bear, say, "Oh, you want your teddy
bear, eh?" This will help her connect the objects to their names and her actions to words.

Describe your own actions. Your baby already thinks you're the most fascinating person alive,
so she'll be engrossed in your every move.

Make it baby's choice

Let your child choose the books she wants you to read to her. Babies often want to hear the
same books over and over again, and they might even start "sight" reading along with you.

Speech and Language Development Milestones *for Toddlers*

2 years

able to use 50 or more words

can put together 2 or 3 words in a simple sentence

may talk in short sentences

understands but may not always follow directions

may talk about events that he remembers happening in the near past, but will confuse words like yesterday and tomorrow

may be able to follow directions using the words "on," "in," and "under"

3 years

may have a 300- to 500- word vocabulary

may lisp or stutter

can tell simple stories

may still struggle with certain consonant sounds, such as using a w sound for r, saying "wabbit" instead of "rabbit," or d for th, saying "dis," "dat," "den," for "this," "that," and "then"

Speech and Language PlaySmart
Activities *for Toddlers*

Toddlers love to take part in adult activities, and they have wild imaginations. You can use both of these new personality traits to work on your child's language skills.

Be a broken record

Repetition is crucial in helping toddlers pick up key words that are a basic part of their day. Repeat short phrases with key words, such as "time to eat" or "where's the ball?"

Read the books your child enjoys over and over again. He'll begin to learn the words, characters, and story on his own.

Reminding your toddler of all the fun he had at the park today will help him connect the words to his real-life experience.

Play pretend

Come up with kid-friendly versions of adult activities, such as a telephone conversation or a doll's lunchtime, to exercise your toddler's word skills as well as his imagination.

Encourage your toddler to read along as you read to him. Of course, he won't actually be reading, but he'll be excited about the activity—an early enjoyment for reading will only inspire him to learn.

Ask questions as you read

Point to pictures in a book and ask your toddler to name them, or vice versa.

Encourage him to jump in when he gets to his favorite part of the story.

Social and Emotional Development
Milestones *for the First Year*

0–3 months

smiles

3–6 months

becomes more active in getting attention

may respond differently to the voice of a stranger than to the voice of a familiar person

will begin to smile at self in the mirror

6–9 months

smiles and laughs upon seeing parent or caregiver

smiles in response to happy-sounding voice

frowns or looks worried in response to angry voice

communicates by using gestures (e.g., reaching out to be picked up)

not as affectionate with unfamiliar people

becomes very upset with strangers

9–12 months

understands the word "no," but doesn't always obey

tries to imitate adult movements (waves, says "bye-bye," blows kisses)

prefers mother to take care of needs

remains hesitant around strangers

Social and Emotional PlaySmart
Activities *for the First Year*

Though they may seem like blobs whose only knowledge is how to eat, sleep, and cry, babies are born with social skills designed to make sure parents feel connected to them—namely, those loving (and heart-melting) gazes and sweet grins. You can help them grow from cute eyelash-flutterers to social butterflies by incorporating some fun group-oriented activities into their day.

Be a goofball

Play silly interactive games with your baby, such as peek-a-boo.

Tickle fests and exaggerated voices will make your baby laugh, and also begin to teach him the difference between playtime and nonplaytime.

Bring your baby to dinner

Literally, even if he hasn't been introduced to solids foods yet. This is a great way for your family to spend quality time together and for your baby to watch as others interact around him.

Address family members, including your baby, by name.

Go out on the town

Whether you're just going grocery shopping or to the post office, a trip outside can be an exciting one for your baby.

Join a playgroup that'll introduce your baby to others. He'll love watching other kids and seeing you interact with people.

Social and Emotional Development
Milestones *for the Second Year*

12–18 months

becomes upset when separated from parent

plays alone on floor with toys

enjoys being held and read to

enjoys an audience and applause

likes to hand objects to others

recognizes self in mirror or pictures

imitates others, especially by coughing, sneezing, or making animal sounds

18–24 months

likes to imitate parents' actions

says "no"

acts very possessive of toys and objects

may get angry sometimes and have temper tantrums

comforts a distressed friend or parent

uses the words "me" and "mine"

tries to do many things "by myself"

enjoys simple pretend play like wearing hats and talking on phone

generally unable to remember rules

shows affection by returning a hug or kiss

begins to show signs of independence

has difficulty sharing

finds it difficult to wait and wants things immediately

acts shy around strangers

refers to self by name

enjoys looking at picture books

enjoys adult attention

enjoys exploring, gets into everything, and requires constant supervision

often gets physically aggressive when frustrated

may become attached to a toy or blanket

Social and Emotional PlaySmart
Activities *for the Second Year*

By their first birthday, babies are starting to feel a sense of independence creeping in. It can be pretty scary for them, which explains their sudden aversion to strangers. While at first she loved meeting new faces at the grocery store, your baby might now become shy and withdrawn around people who aren't mom or dad.

New people, new places

Set up play dates with other kids, including trips to the park and the zoo.

Give your baby some warm-up time when she's in a new environment, and let her stay right by your side.

Let her hang on to her pacifier or toy so she's as comfortable as possible.

Show her she's not the only kid on the block

Take your baby to the playground, which will introduce her to a whole world of little kids just like herself.

She may not actually communicate with other children yet, but instead play side-by-side. The more exposure she has with others her age, the sooner she'll start to interact.

Me, me, me, and me

Your baby wants constant attention, so give her as much as possible. But know when to step away.

With her newfound confidence and independent streak, your baby will probably love to help around the house. So give her simple jobs, such as carrying a small pile of laundry or helping to make her bed.

Social and Emotional Development
Milestones *for Toddlers*

2–3 years

shows more interest in other children

begins to learn how to share

uses the word "mine" often

understands gender

likes a daily routine and wants to know what it is

begins to understand rules that are consistently reinforced

can be cooperative in simple games with other children

becomes better with transitions from one activity to the next

can identify self in the mirror

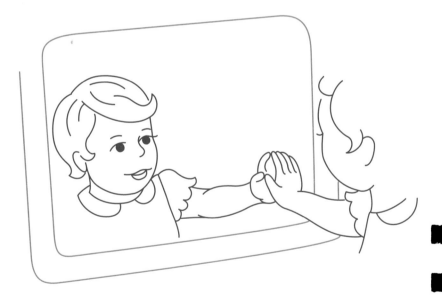

Social and Emotional PlaySmart
Activities *for Toddlers*

This is a confusing time for your child: She feels more independent than ever, but then sometimes reverts to full-on baby mode. She wants to act like her mom and dad, but still wants the cuddling and affection she's always had. Being gentle but firm with your toddler will go a long way in teaching her the ins and outs of the big-kid world.

Teach self-control

Practice sharing by playing games that'll offer both you and your child a turn.

Encourage your child to be patient and wait until it's her turn to play, respond, or act.

Find (and keep) playmates

Slowly, your child will go from parallel play to engaging with other children. The more she's around others, the more she'll learn how to be part of a group.

Let her hang out with older kids to give her other people besides Mom and Dad to look up to and learn from.

Encourage "big-kid" behavior

Set up a low-level bookshelf or box of books on the floor so your toddler can select her own book to read and can flip through the pages herself.

Have your toddler help clean up her toys, make her bed, and participate in adult household chores.

Cognitive Development Milestones
for the First Year

0–3 months

differentiates the scent of mother from all others

begins to recognize patterns, e.g., the presence of a bottle means feeding time

sees clearly about 8 inches (20 cm), but not much farther than that

sees high contrasts

3–6 months

focuses on objects 15 feet (3 m) away

can tell colors apart

has better depth perception

6–9 months

can differentiate even subtle colors

repeats an action over and over, observing that actions have effects

explores the world by putting everything in the mouth

9–12 months

drops objects to listen to and compare the sound each one makes

goes around, under, or over things to reach desired objects

can sit and look at a simple picture book

Cognitive PlaySmart Activities

for the First Year

What might be a game to you is actually a learning experience for your baby. "Playtime" is a crucial cognitive exercise for kids, whether they're using their imagination or their problem-solving skills.

Play the same games again and again, and again

Play hiding games like peek-a-boo and hide-and-seek over and over again. The repetition will teach your baby that objects and parents don't cease to exist when she can't see them.

Sing interactive songs that include tickles or hand motions, such as "This Little Piggy" and "The Itsy-Bitsy Spider." As she gets older, she'll know exactly when to expect the tickle attack, but it'll be no less hilarious and exciting for her.

If your baby can't clap yet, gently lead her in a game of pat-a-cake by holding her hands. By 3 years of age, your child will want to make up her own version and teach it to you.

Play with sounds and colors

Give your baby bright, multicolored toys to play with—whether they're stacking rings or rattles or teething rings.

Drop various objects into a plastic container and let her hear the different sounds they make. At first, you'll be the one dropping the objects, but soon your baby will be the one insisting on what gets dropped.

Cognitive Development Milestones

for the Second Year

12–18 months

goes after a hidden object

spends more time exploring an object

wants to turn pages of books

can match two objects together by color, shape, or size

pays more attention to the actions of others, and may try to imitate those actions, like feeding or changing a doll

18–24 months

knows "scripted" routines, e.g., getting ready for bed means brushing teeth, putting on pajamas, reading a story

understands past, present, and future

expects objects to be in "proper" places, e.g., a toy in a toy box or milk in the refrigerator

Cognitive PlaySmart Activities
for the Second Year

Every part of the day is a learning opportunity for your baby, so turn mundane adult tasks into kid-friendly activities—whether it's talking on the telephone, cooking, or cleaning up.

Sort and organize

Your baby will flex his problem-solving skills with toys that require "sorting." Shape sorters or stacking cups are great examples.

Have him put his own toys away into a toy chest or box. Then cross your fingers that he'll always be this willing to clean up after himself. (Outlook: doubtful.)

Play pretend

Let your child participate in exciting grown-up activities, such as drying a just-washed plastic cup as you do dishes. Well, they're exciting to him.

Get him a toy telephone or toy cooking equipment to use while you're doing the real thing.

"Act out" songs

Teach your baby songs that are meant to be acted out, such as "I'm a Little Teapot," "Head, Shoulders, Knees, and Toes," and "The Itsy-Bitsy Spider." You'll probably have to do a lot of the "acting," but soon your baby will be piping up himself.

Cognitive Development Milestones
for Toddlers

2–3 years

understands simple stories

can match familiar items to pictures of those items

may "play house," using familiar household objects appropriately

can put toys or objects into categories

understands gender differences

may play pretend with dolls and stuffed animals

names pictures of objects and points to pictures of people doing familiar activities in books

counts "1-2-3" and understands number-item correspondence

can do simple jigsaw puzzles (2 to 4 pieces)

Cognitive PlaySmart Activities
for Toddlers

Toddlers have a stronger sense of themselves than younger children. They'll need activities that are a little more challenging.

Make it a challenge

Toys that require assembling objects, such as puzzles or building blocks, are an excellent challenge for toddlers. They'll feel triumphant when their masterpiece is completed, and then promptly tear it down again.

Toys and games that teach the ABCs and 123s and involve picture-matching are also tons of fun and educational.

Role-playing remains a popular and educational activity for your toddler. If she lets you, jump in and participate.

Read books your toddler can relate to

Your child will love hearing stories about kids her age, and better yet, seeing pictures of kids her age.

Help her connect activities in the story to activities she's experienced herself—whether the story takes her to the zoo, a park, or for a drive in the car.

Chapter 5

Healthy Baby

Prevention and
Common Ailments

Chapter 5 **Healthy Baby**

HEALTHY BABY

You cannot (and should not) avoid all illness. Once your kid begins to socialize, you will discover that children are germ vectors, unconcernedly spreading viruses from one wet, sticky little person to another, and, all too often, to parents, too. This is as it must be. Kids' immune systems develop by battling viruses, bacteria, and other entities. So get used to it! Learn to treat common ailments and when to recognize that you need a professional opinion. Oh, and you might want to stock up on tissues, too.

Basic Baby-Care

Get to know your pediatrician. Don't be afraid to be that parent who takes a child to the doctor for every little thing. Your pediatrician should be like a member of your extended family during the first few years of baby's life. Symptoms of any kind that are sudden, persistent, or worsening should be brought to the attention of your pediatrician as soon as possible.

When you call about your baby's symptoms, one of the first questions your pediatrician will likely ask is "Does she have a temperature?" Most pediatricians will recommend that you use only a rectal thermometer for babies 3 months and younger. After that, you can use a thermometer that works either in the ear or armpit. You can determine the margin of error by taking your child's temperature when she is not sick. Tell the doctor what kind of thermometer you used. Please note that you should not use an oral thermometer until your child is 4 or 5 years of age.

Immunization shots are a big part of your child's doctor visits during the first 3 years, and they are harder on you than your baby for more than one reason. This becomes apparent the first time you take your baby to the doctor for shots: the sight of her hysteria—however brief it may be—is so convincing that it could bring even the manliest man to tears.

Parents need to monitor their child's reaction to a particular shot or group of shots. Parents should also feel comfortable asking questions and know what their options are (because there are options). So gather as much accurate information about each shot as you can. (The information you'll find on the Internet doesn't count unless it comes from a reliable site.) Generally, most kids should and will get their immunization shots, although some parents choose to avoid certain shots for medical, religious, or otherwise personal reasons. But you should get your facts straight before making your decision.

Know Your Medications

Medicate as prescribed by your pediatrician and by the medication's packaging. Let's state this for the record: Antibiotics CANNOT treat a viral infection of any kind. Doctors will prescribe an antibiotic to fight a BACTERIAL infection only. Cough and cold medicines have been taken off the market for children younger than 2 years of age, due to questionable effectiveness and concerns about overdosing. Your remaining options are acetaminophen and ibuprofen for fever, antihistamines such as Benadryl for allergies, and home remedies such as honey for coughs (never give honey to a child younger than 1 year old). Avoid combination medications (those treating multiple symptoms, such as cough/allergy). Before giving your child any medicine, check with your pediatrician.

Never give a child aspirin or salicylates, particularly when a viral illness such as chicken pox or respiratory influenza is present, as it has been linked to the deadly Reye's syndrome. In general, aspirin should not be taken by anyone under the age of 20 unless prescribed by a doctor.

An Ounce of Prevention

Wash your hands. Wash your hands. Wash your hands. Any questions? Washing your hands regularly and thoroughly is the best way to prevent the transmission of illness. Wash them after using the toilet or changing a diaper, when you come in from outdoors, before you handle food or eat, and whenever it's been a while since you last washed them. Insist that anyone who wants to hold your newborn washes hands first.

Baby-proof your home before your baby goes mobile. You might even want to do it before the baby is born, when you actually have some time. After your baby is home from the hospital, the task of baby-proofing falls somewhere between getting more sleep and changing the light bulbs. You'll get around to it later, but "later" becomes next month, and next month becomes too late.

Medicine Cabinet Checklist
Birth – Toddlerhood

You'll want these basic items on hand:

- [ ] digital thermometer, rectal and ear or armpit
- [ ] bulb syringe or nasal aspirator (aka "snot sucker")
- [ ] rubbing alcohol
- [ ] diaper ointment with zinc oxide
- [ ] petroleum jelly or lanolin
- [ ] antibiotic ointment
- [ ] infant drops and children's liquid acetaminophen (such as Tylenol)
- [ ] infant drops and children's liquid ibuprofen (such as Advil or Motrin)
- [ ] children's formula antihistamine (such as Benadryl)
- [ ] 0.5% hydrocortisone cream
- [ ] tweezers
- [ ] baby sunscreen
- [ ] child-safe insect repellent
- [ ] adhesive bandage strips
- [ ] sterile gauze pads and rolls
- [ ] first-aid tape

How to Take an Infant's Temperature

It's not easy to determine whether your baby is seriously ill or not—that's why parents should be on their toes when they notice any sign of fever or illness. Feel your baby's head to get a quick gauge on a fever, then take his temperature using a rectal thermometer—yep, until they invent a less squirm-inducing method, rectal is still the most accurate way to go (ew). Don't use the thermometer on any other body parts, or right after your baby's eaten or taken a bath.

▨ Wipe the tip of the thermometer with rubbing alcohol to sterilize, and then coat it with a thin layer of petroleum jelly.

▨ Lay baby on his back on a towel (he may poop when you remove the thermometer). If there are two of you (ideal), one can try to distract baby with a toy, while the other performs the temp reading.

▨ Holding the thermometer in one hand, spread baby's butt cheeks with the other and gently insert the tip of the thermometer into his rectum no more than a fingertip's length.

▨ Hold baby's butt cheeks together until the thermometer beeps. Remove and note temperature.

▨ Clean, dry, and store thermometer in a safe place for next time.

DO NOT USE

- **Mercury Thermometers**: These are considered hazardous waste—call your local sanitation department for instructions on how to dispose of them.

- **Forehead Strips**: They are simply inaccurate.

- **Oral Thermometers**: Do not use for children under 4 years.

- **Ear Thermometers**: Do not use alone if fever is above 102 degrees F or 39 degrees C. Test again with an oral or rectal thermometer.

Defining and Treating a Fever

Fever is cause for concern but not for undue worry. It is a symptom, not an illness itself, and tells you that your child's immune system is doing its job. Babies under 3 months, however, have immature immune systems, so any fever over 100.4 degrees F or 40 degrees C warrants an immediate call to the doctor. For older babies and toddlers with a fever, behavior is a major clue to what you should do: If your child looks well, is playing, eating, and seems generally happy, there is no need to call the doctor. If she looks ill and seems lethargic or unduly miserable, go ahead and make the call. Treat a fever with ibuprofen or acetaminophen; if the fever does not respond within an hour of administering the medicine, call the doctor.

FAHRENHEIT	CELSIUS	DESCRIPTION
104	40	**HIGH**
103.2	39.6	**HIGH**
102.2	39	Medium
101.4	38.6	Medium
100.4	38	Low
99.6	37.6	Low
98.6	37	Normal

TREATMENT

Give appropriate dose of acetaminophen or ibuprofen (see Chart 5.9 or 5.11). For a very high or persistent fever, these drugs can be alternated— ask your pediatrican.

When to Call the Doctor

As a new parent, you may be fighting the urge to call the doctor all the time. Or in trying not to be a neurotic parent, maybe you're playing down baby's symptoms while your spouse freaks out. Eventually, you will learn to trust your instincts. Until then, use this checklist as a guide. (See also Chart 6.1: Your First Aid Kit on page 106.)

Call the doctor immediately if your baby or toddler experiences any of these symptoms:

☐ Very irritable, or crying inconsolably

☐ Confusion

☐ Lethargic (doctors define this as limp, unresponsive, or difficult to awaken)

☐ Medium to high fever that has not responded an hour after treatment with acetaminophen or ibuprofen

☐ Fever over 101 degrees F (38 degrees C) that lasts more than 5 days, or over 103 degrees F (39 degrees C) lasting longer than 3 days

☐ Persistent vomiting lasting more than 3 days

☐ Dehydration (peeing less than once in 6 to 8 hours, no tears when crying, dry mouth, sunken eyes)

☐ Difficulty breathing (rapid, hard breathing; if you can see his ribs or shoulders moving with the breaths, or it seems like he cannot catch his breath)

☐ Rash accompanied by fever

☐ Persistent or severe pain

☐ Convulsion or seizure (unusual stiffness or floppiness)

☐ Bloody stool without constipation or diarrhea

Common Childhood Ailments Tummy Troubles

A baby's digestive system is delicate, so monitoring your baby's feeding and pooping schedule will help you catch any bellyaches at the start. Watch out for the symptoms below.

Constipation

SYMPTOMS Hard, painful stools; toddlers going 4+ days without a bowel movement; infants with hard, dry poop pellets

CAUSE Dietary changes; lack of fiber in diet; insufficient fluids

TREATMENT Change diet; add prunes; add fiber and fluids; laxative; enema

TYPICAL DURATION Varies

CALL DOCTOR IF . . . Problem persists or becomes chronic

Diarrhea

SYMPTOMS Frequent, watery stools; sometimes with loss of appetite, vomiting, low fever

CAUSE Dietary changes; viral or bacterial intestinal infection; food intolerance or sensitivity; allergy

TREATMENT Change diet; give fluids; BRATY diet (bananas, rice, applesauce, toast—dry, yogurt); Popsicles

TYPICAL DURATION Up to a week

CALL DOCTOR IF . . . Bloody diarrhea; dehydration; lethargy; weight loss; increased abdominal pain

Urinary Tract Infection

SYMPTOMS Fever; painful urination; odd-smelling, cloudy, or bloody pee

CAUSE Bacterial infection in the urinary tract

TREATMENT Antibiotics; fluids (try cranberry juice)

TYPICAL DURATION 3 to 7 days

CALL DOCTOR IF . . . Baby exhibits any of these symptoms

Gastroesophageal Reflux

SYMPTOMS More than usual spitting up, coughing, or gagging during feeding, reduced appetite, failure to gain weight, nighttime cough, sinus, or ear infections

CAUSE Weak esophageal sphincter allows food and gastric juices to flow back up from the stomach

TREATMENT Smaller, more frequent feedings; keep baby upright; antacids or acid-blocking medication

TYPICAL DURATION Usually resolves by 12 months

CALL DOCTOR IF . . . Baby loses weight

Common Childhood Ailments Skin and Eyes

Every kid gets something; soon you will be an expert on what your child has had and can impress the parents of kids who haven't had it yet! For each of these common skin and eye ailments, the first time will be the scariest—see your pediatrician to get the diagnosis, treatment, and reassurance you'll need.

Conjunctivitis

SYMPTOMS Red, itchy eyes; green or yellow discharge from eyes

CAUSE Virus or bacteria; allergies; highly contagious (keep linens and towels separate)

TREATMENT Clean eyes with damp cloth or cotton ball; use warm compress, saline or antibiotic eyedrops or ointment (be sure to finish)

TYPICAL DURATION 3 to 5 days

CALL DOCTOR IF . . . Symptoms persist after 5 days of treatment

Blocked Tear Duct

SYMPTOMS Yellow discharge, often from one eye only

CAUSE Membrane blocking tear duct

TREATMENT Gently massage area on side of nose; clean discharge with clean cloth and sterile water

TYPICAL DURATION Newborns— 6 months

CALL DOCTOR IF . . . Eye looks red and swollen or discharge increases

88

Diaper Rash

SYMPTOMS Rashes in the diaper area and red, tender skin around it

CAUSE Prolonged contact with urine or feces in the diaper; not contagious

TREATMENT More frequent diaper changes, ointment containing zinc oxide, air on the area (e.g., go without diaper)

TYPICAL DURATION A few days

CALL DOCTOR IF . . . Rash does not respond to treatment; skin becomes raw

Eczema

SYMPTOMS Patches of dry, itchy, thickened skin that may "weep" clear fluid and crust or scale over

CAUSE Allergies, dry skin, food sensitivities; not contagious

TREATMENT Moisturize skin, avoid triggers, steroid creams—see Chart 1.9

TYPICAL DURATION This very common condition may flare up and recede through childhood and beyond

CALL DOCTOR IF . . . Skin becomes terribly irritated or infected

Cradle Cap

SYMPTOMS Yellow or brown greasy scales or crusting on the scalp

CAUSE Overactive sebaceous glands

TREATMENT Massage with apricot oil and gently brush out scales; wash with mild anti-dandruff shampoo; prescription creams

TYPICAL DURATION Extremely common, appears in first 6 weeks, often disappears by 9 months

CALL DOCTOR IF . . . Skin becomes very irritated or scales spread to other areas of body

Impetigo

SYMPTOMS Small red blisters that quickly turn into honey-colored crusts

CAUSE Streptococcus or staphyloccus bacteria; highly contagious

TREATMENT Antibiotic ointments, oral antibiotics

TYPICAL DURATION 3 to 7 days

CALL DOCTOR IF . . . Does not respond to treatment; fever or red streaks develop

Common Childhood Ailments Fevers

Fevers are very common in babies, and mostly harmless. However, if your child's fever is accompanied by any of the symptoms listed below, it may be much more serious and require medical attention.

Coxsackievirus/Herpangina

SYMPTOMS

High fever; no appetite; sore throat; blisters in mouth, throat, on hands and feet, and in diaper area

CAUSE

Virus; highly contagious

TREATMENT

Acetaminophen or ibuprofen; fluids; rest

TYPICAL DURATION

3 to 6 days

CALL DOCTOR IF . . .

Fever lasts more than 5 days; signs of dehydration

Roseola *(Sixth Disease, Roseola Infantum, or Exanthem Subitum)*

SYMPTOMS

High fever lasting 3 to 7 days, followed by red rash that starts on the trunk and spreads; may have cold or flu symptoms

CAUSE

Virus (HHV); highly contagious

TREATMENT

Acetaminophen or ibuprofen; fluids; rest

TYPICAL DURATION

3 to 7 days of fever; 3 days to 3 weeks of rash

CALL DOCTOR IF . . .

Fever does not respond to treatment

Fifth Disease *(Erythema Infectiosum, Slapped Cheek Disease)*

SYMPTOMS
Bright red cheeks, pale mouth; low fever; possible lacy, itchy rash on trunk

CAUSE
Parvovirus; highly contagious, with particular risk to pregnant women

TREATMENT
Acetaminophen or ibuprofen; Benadryl for itching

TYPICAL DURATION
2 to 5 days, rash may last or recur for months

CALL DOCTOR IF . . .
Child has anemia or immune disorder

Chicken Pox

SYMPTOMS
Fever; red, itchy bumps that blister then crust

CAUSE
Varicella virus; highly contagious

TREATMENT
Acetaminophen or ibuprofen if fever is high; oatmeal baths or Benadryl for itching

TYPICAL DURATION
About a week

CALL DOCTOR IF . . .
Blisters form on eyelids; spots become infected; accompanied by serious cough, dizziness, headaches, or stiff neck; fever persists 5 or more days

A Cold, the Flu, or Something Else?

How to Tell

Upper respiratory viruses, including the common cold, cause all sorts of unpleasantness, and occasionally complications that require a visit to the doctor. In that case, here are some new parent vocabulary words that you may need to know:

RETRACTIONS if baby's breathing is labored and you can see the muscles in the neck or around the ribs being sucked in

STRIDOR high-pitched whistling sounds when inhaling

WHEEZING high-pitched whistling noises when exhaling

AILMENT	SYMPTOMS	CAUSE
Cold	Runny or stuffy nose, sore throat, low-grade fever, cough, slightly decreased appetite	Virus; contagious
Flu	Sudden onset of fever (often high), headache, fatigue, nausea/vomiting, diarrhea, plus cold symptoms	Virus; contagious
Croup	Barking cough, stridor, often preceded by cold symptoms	Virus; bacteria, or allergy causing swelling of larynx and trachea; narrowing of breathing passages
Ear/Sinus Infection	Cold symptoms that do not improve, followed by cough, fever, pain in face or ear, green mucus	Bacterial infection, usually a complication of a respiratory virus
Pneumonia	Persistent cold symptoms followed by cough, high fever, rapid breathing, stridor, retractions, loss of appetite, decreased activity, chest pain, sore throat, headache	Virus; bacteria; fungi

TREATMENT	TYPICAL DURATION	CALL DOCTOR IF...
Fluids, rest, steam, acetaminophen for fever	10 days to 3 weeks	Symptoms worsen after 5 days
Fluids, rest, steam, acetaminophen for fever	3 days to 2 weeks	Symptoms persist or worsen
Steam, cold air, steroids	3 to 4 days	Child has difficulty breathing, including retractions, stridor, blue tint around mouth, difficulty swallowing, high fever
For mild cases, same as cold; for more severe cases, antibiotics may be prescribed	7 to 10 days; must finish antibiotics	Symptoms persist
If cause is not viral, antibiotics may be prescribed	5 to 10 days	Child has difficulty breathing, turns bluish around mouth or fingertips, or has fever that does not respond to treatment

Acetaminophen *Infant Dosages*

Acetaminophen is a fever reducer and pain reliever that's considered very safe for infants and children at the recommended dosages. Another plus: It causes fewer stomach upsets than ibuprofen (aka Advil or Motrin). Acetaminophen usually kicks in within 45 to 60 minutes, but if you don't see any improvement, call your pediatrician for advice. Look for the brand name Tylenol.

WEIGHT*	INFANT DROPS	CHILDREN'S LIQUID	CHEWABLE TABLETS 80 MG TABS
6 to 11 lbs (2.7 to 5 kg)	0.4 ml (½ dropper)	—	—
12 to 17 lbs (5.5 to 7.7 kg)	0.8 ml (1 dropper)	½ tsp	—
18 to 23 lbs (8.2 to 10.5 kg)	1.2 ml (1½ droppers)	¾ tsp (3.75 ml)	—
24 to 35 lbs (10.9 to 15.9 kg)	1.6 ml (2 droppers)	1 tsp (5 ml)	2 tablets

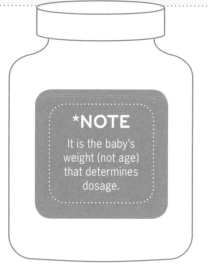

*NOTE

It is the baby's weight (not age) that determines dosage.

Benadryl *Infant Dosages*

Benadryl, or diphenhydramine, is an antihistamine that reduces the itching, sneezing, swelling, and rash caused by an allergic reaction, and it's safe for 1-year-olds and up. Benadryl sometimes causes drowsiness, but it can also have the opposite effect, arousing or stimulating a child. And note that antihistamines are known to cause dry mouth.

WEIGHT	LIQUID 12.5 MG/5 ML	CHEWABLE TABLETS 12.5 MG EACH	TABLETS 25 MG EACH
17 to 21 lbs (7.7 to 9.5 kg)	¾ tsp (3.75 ml)	Use liquid	Use liquid
22 to 32 lbs (10 to 14.5 kg)	1 tsp (5 ml)	1 tablet	Use liquid or chews
33 to 42 lbs (15 to 19 kg)	1½ tsp (7.5 ml)	1½ tablets	Use liquid or chews
43 to 53 lbs (19.5 to 24 kg)	2 tsp (10 ml)	2 tablets	1 tablet

Ibuprofen *Infant Dosages*

Ibuprofen, an anti-inflammatory that lowers fever and relieves pain, is safe for babies 2 months and up. Don't administer ibuprofen if your baby has an upset or empty stomach. It usually kicks in within 30 minutes. Brand names include Advil, Motrin, and Pediacare.

WEIGHT	MILLIGRAM DOSAGE	PEDIACARE DROPS 50 MG/1.25 ML	ADVIL/MOTRIN DROPS 50 MG/1.25 ML
9 to 10 lbs (4 to 4.5 kg)	25 mg	½ dropper (0.625 ml)	⅓ syringe (0.625 ml)
11 to 16 lbs (5 to 7. 2 kg)	50 mg	1 dropper (1.25 ml)	⅔ syringe (1.25 ml)
17 to 21 lbs (7.7 to 9.5 kg)	75 mg	1½ droppers (1.25 ml + 0.625 ml)	1 syringe (1.875 ml)
22 to 26 lbs (10 to 11.8 kg)	100 mg	2 droppers (2 x 1.25 ml)	1⅓ syringe (1.875 ml + 0.625 ml)
27 to 32 lbs (12.2 to 14.5 kg)	125 mg	2½ droppers (2 x 1.25 ml + 0.625 ml)	1⅔ syringe (1.875 ml + 01.25 ml)
33 to 37 lbs (15 to 16.8 kg)	150 mg	3 droppers (3 x 1.25 ml)	2 syringes (2 x 1.875 ml)
38 to 42 lbs (17.2 to 19 kg)	175 mg	3½ droppers (3 x 1.25 ml + 0.625 ml)	2⅓ syringes (2 x 1.875 ml + 0.625 ml)
43 to 53 lbs (19.5 to 24 kg)	200 mg	4 droppers (4 x 1.25 ml)	2⅔ syringes (2 x 1.875 ml + 1.25 ml)

NOTE ON DROPPER SIZES

- **Pediacare Fever Drops** 1.25 ml (¼ tsp) dropper (½ dropper = 0.625 ml and 1 full dropper = 1.25 ml)

- **Motrin and Advil Infant Drops** 1.875 ml syringe (⅓ syringe = 0.625 ml, ⅔ syringe = 1.25 ml, and 1 syringe = 1.875 ml)

- Don't let the dropper/syringe difference confuse you. The milligram amount you're giving is the same, you're just using a different-sized container.

CHILDREN'S LIQUID 100 MG/5 ML	CHEWABLE TABLETS 50 MG EACH	JUNIOR STRENGTH CAPS OR CHEWS 100 MG EACH
N/A	N/A	N/A
½ tsp (2.5 ml)	N/A	N/A
¾ tsp (3.75 ml)	N/A	N/A
1 tsp (5 ml)	2 tablets	1 tablet
1¼ tsp (6.25 ml)	2½ tablets	N/A
1½ tsp (7.5 ml)	3 tablets	1½ tablets
1¾ tsp (8.75 ml)	3½ tablets	N/A
2 tsp (10 ml)	4 tablets	2 tablets

Immunization Schedule

This chart is based on the Centers for Disease Control and Prevention's recommendations; you and your pediatrician should decide together how to proceed.

AGE	Birth to 2 months	1 to 4 months	2 months
VACCINE	Hepatitis B Hib Polio (IPV) Pneumococcal (PVC) Rotavirus	Hepatitis B Hib Polio (IPV) Pneumococcal (PVC) Rotavirus	DTaP Hib Pneumococcal (PVC) Rotavirus

12 to 15 months	12 to 18 months	12 to 23 months	15 to 18 months
Hib MMR Pneumococcal (PVC)	Hepatitis B	Hepatitis A	DTaP

Immunization Glossary

What are these immunizations for exactly?

DTAP	diphtheria, tetanus, and pertussis (aka whooping cough)
HEPATITIS A	Hepatitis (liver disease)
HEPATITIS B (HBV)	Hepatitis (liver disease)
HIB	Haemophilus influenza type B, which can lead to meningitits, pneumonia, and epiglottitis
HPV	human papillomavirus, a common sexually transmitted disease and a cause of cervical cancer
INFLUENZA	flu

4 months	6 months	6 to 18 months
DTaP Polio (IPV) Pneumococcal (PVC)	DTaP MMR	Hepatitis B

2 to 6 years	4 to 6 years	11 to 12 years
Hepatitis A MMR	Polio (IPV) Meningococcal (MCV4) HPV (girls)	Tdap (DtaP booster)

MENINGOCOCCAL	Meningococcal disease, a common cause of meningitis in children
MMR	measles, mumps, and rubella
PNEUMOCOCCAL (PCV)	Pneumococcal disease, a common cause of meningitis, pneumonia, and ear infections
POLIO (IPV)	Polio
ROTAVIRUS	a common cause of severe diarrhea, vomiting, fever, and dehydration (oral vaccination, not injection)
VARICELLA	chicken pox

How to Wash Hands

Washing your hands is your first and most important weapon in the battle against disease. You may think you know all about it, but good hand-washing technique is actually quite rare. The Centers for Disease Control and Prevention provide a clear set of instructions. Follow them yourself and teach your kids.

WHEN SHOULD YOU WASH YOUR HANDS?

Before preparing or eating food

After using the bathroom

After changing diapers or cleaning up a child who has gone to the bathroom

Before and after tending to someone who is sick

After blowing your nose, coughing, or sneezing

After handling garbage

After handling an animal or animal waste

Before and after treating a cut or wound

HOW TO WASH HANDS WITH SOAP AND WATER

1 Thoroughly wet your hands with clean running water. Use warm water if it is available

2 Apply soap. Use as much as you need to create a lather

3 Rub hands together to make a lather and scrub all surfaces, including between the fingers, palms, backs of hands, and fingernails

4 Continue rubbing hands for 20 seconds. Need a timer? Imagine singing "Happy Birthday" twice

5 Rinse hands well under running water until all soap is washed away

6 Dry your hands using a paper towel or air dryer. If possible, use your paper towel to turn off the faucet. In a public restroom, you may also wish to use it to open the door.

IF SOAP AND WATER ARE NOT AVAILABLE

1 Use an alcohol-based gel

2 Apply product to the palm of one hand

3 Rub hands together

4 Rub the product over all surfaces of hands and fingers until hands are dry

Source: Centers for Disease Control and Prevention, United States Department of Health and Human Services

Babyproofing Checklist *Room-by-Room*

Start the process of babyproofing your home by getting down on your hands and knees and crawling around each room. You will be astonished and probably horrified at all the hazards you'll see at an infant's level, from loose and/or small objects that can be swallowed to unstable bookcases to frayed wires, not to mention cat food (mmm, tasty) and humongous dust bunnies (ahh-choo!).

ALL ROOMS

☐ Secure all drapery and blind cords out of reach to prevent strangulation.

☐ Install window stops so windows open no more than 4 inches (10 cm).

☐ Install sturdy, secure window guards to prevent falls.

☐ Ensure screens are securely attached and cannot be pushed out.

☐ Cover all child-accessible outlets with outlet covers that cannot be removed by a child.

☐ Wind up and secure excess appliance cords.

☐ Use power strip safety covers.

☐ Keep vaporizers, humidifiers, floor fans, and portable heaters out of baby's reach.

☐ Remove potentially toxic substances (alcoholic beverages, cleaning supplies, etc.) from lower cabinets and move them to an upper latched cabinet.

DOORS AND CLOSETS

☐ Install one-piece doorstops instead of the kind with rubber tips, which can easily be removed and are choking hazards.

☐ Install unreachable locks or doorknob covers on rooms or closets that you don't want your child to enter.

☐ Lockable interior doors must be unlockable from both sides (to prevent lock-ins).

☐ Install childproof locks on doors to the outside to prevent your child from leaving.

☐ Immediately remove dry cleaning bags; tie each into a knot and put in an inaccessible trash can.

STAIRWAYS, BALCONIES, AND DECK

☐ Mount gates at the top and bottom of stairs to prevent falls.

☐ Make sure gaps between rails and banisters are less than 4 inches (10 cm).

☐ Install acrylic sheeting around railings to prevent falling through or getting stuck in the spaces between railings.

BATHROOM

☐ Install safety latches on all cabinets and drawers; store all toiletries, appliances, and accessories inside.

☐ Lower water heater thermostat to 120 degrees F (49 degrees C) to prevent scalding.

☐ Put a toilet lock on the toilet lid.

☐ Install a lock on the medicine cabinet.

BABY'S ROOM

☐ Get a crib that meets current safety standards.

☐ If you must use an old crib, be sure crib slat spacing is $2\frac{3}{8}$ inches (5.9 cm) or less, has no lead paint, and otherwise meets modern safety standards.

☐ Place crib away from window and window treatments.

☐ Set the crib mattress to the appropriate position so baby cannot stand and fall or climb out.

☐ Remove mobile over crib when baby reaches 5 months or can push up on hands and knees.

☐ Leave bedding, stuffed toys, or hanging objects out of infant's crib—wait until baby is 1 year.

☐ Install and use safety belt on changing table.

☐ Keep changing accessories out of infant's reach but within yours.

☐ Crib mattress must be firm and fit snugly into crib.

☐ Crib sheets must fit tightly.

Babyproofing Checklist *Room-by-Room*

LIVING AREAS

☐ Remove or permanently affix to walls heavy appliances (such as televisions) that could fall over on a child.

☐ Use metal brackets to attach all storage units, bookcases, dressers, armoires, or bureaus to the walls. Store heavy items on bottom shelf.

☐ Install drawer guards on accessible drawers or remove dangerous items.

☐ Check the undersides of chairs and tables for protruding nails or screws.

☐ Tighten loose knobs on cabinets and drawers.

☐ Remove or make inaccessible all plants (babies will eat dirt, and many plants are toxic).

☐ Pad sharp edges on tables and chests.

☐ Replace glass tabletops with unbreakables.

KITCHEN

☐ Install safety latches on all cabinets and drawers.

☐ Install a guard or remove knobs from the front of the stove.

☐ Use back burners when possible and keep pot handles facing the back of the stove.

☐ Keep hot foods away from table and counter edges.

☐ Never carry or hold your baby and hot liquids (such as a cup of coffee) or foods at the same time.

☐ Keep all appliances closed and locked, including dishwasher, oven, trash compactor, and garbage and recycling containers.

☐ Remove small magnets from refrigerator; they are choking hazards.

☐ Tie up and toss out plastic grocery bags immediately.

☐ Remove countertop knife holders.

☐ Always use high chair safety strap.

Booboo Baby

First Aid

Chapter 6   **Booboo Baby**

BOOBOO BABY

Chances are, your baby is going to have more than a few "owies" during those first few years. The trick is to be as prepared as possible. Have your first aid kit stocked and ready for absolutely anything. Take an infant CPR course (and see our CPR instructions on pages 121–124 of the Appendix) and keep your skills up to date. Insist that caregivers also be certified in infant CPR and resuscitation.

Hot! Don't touch!

The most frequent household culprits in burn accidents are liquids, whether from super-hot faucets, steam, or spilled coffee. Do all you can to keep scalding liquids and dangerous appliances out of your child's reach. Any burn merits a call to the doctor; for a serious burn, call for emergency medical attention immediately.

Stings and Bites

The most dangerous insect perpetrators are bees, wasps, hornets, yellow jackets, and fire ants, but mosquitoes, ticks, biting flies, and some spiders also can cause reactions. All animal and human bites require a response. Animals may transmit rabies, and all bites carry a risk of infection. Be sure your child's tetanus immunization is up to date. (See Chart 6.4: Animal or Human Bites on page 109 for treatment.)

Choking

Babies explore the world by touching things and sticking them in their mouths. Unfortunately, babies also have really little pipes—and even the tiniest morsels of food can get caught inside them. To prevent your child from swallowing something that shouldn't be swallowed, make sure these objects aren't within reach. Read toy packaging before opening to find out whether its parts are small enough to fit in your baby's mouth. And don't let dangerously sized foods such as popcorn, grapes, and baby carrots cross your child's path until he's 4 years old.

Bumps, Bruises, and Scrapes

When your baby takes a tumble, he'll probably panic more from the shock of a fall than from any pain. So it's your job to be cool, collected, and quick to check for serious booboos. If there is obvious swelling or a deformity in the extremities, or if the child is limping for more than a few hours, you should call your doctor or go to the ER.

Your First Aid Kit

Keep it handy. You might consider keeping a spare in each car, as well.

NONMEDICINE ITEMS

☐ First aid manual   ☐ Heating pad   ☐ Nonlatex gloves

☐ Sterilized cotton balls or pads   ☐ Adhesive tape—to secure the gauze

☐ Small flashlight for checking ears, nose, throat, and eyes

☐ Scissors with rounded tips—for cutting tape

☐ Alcohol pads—to clean instruments like scissors, thermometer, or tweezers

☐ Adhesive bandage strips in various sizes and shapes—choose a gentle, less-sticky type for children's skin

☐ Gauze pads and/or rolls—for cuts that are odd sizes; consider gauze rolls ½ to 2 inches (1 to 5 cm) wide as well as 2-inch-square and 4-inch-square (5- or 10-cm-square) pads

☐ Elastic bandages, such as ACE wraps—for wrapping sprained joints or making a sling for a broken arm, wrist, or hand

CUTS/SCRAPES

☐ Hydrogen peroxide—to clean cuts and scrapes

☐ Mild liquid soap or prepackaged baby-safe cleansing wipes—to clean minor scrapes

☐ Antibacterial cream and/or antibiotic ointment—to minimize infections in cuts and scrapes

ALLERGIC REACTIONS

☐ Diphenhydramine (Benadryl) in infant or children's formulas—for minor allergic reactions and certain emergencies; consult your provider for use and dosage

☐ Self-injectable epinephrine, if prescribed—for children with life-threatening allergic reactions from certain foods or insect bites

RASHES/BUG BITES

☐ Topical calamine lotion—relieves minor itching due to poison ivy, rashes, or insect bites

☐ Hydrocortisone cream—used for rashes or insect bites

☐ Topical antihistamine lotion or stick, to apply directly onto the bite or rash

POISON RESPONSE

If you suspect your baby has ingested anything unsafe, immediately call poison control and follow the instructions you receive. Do not home treat without medical advice.

Burns

All burns can be avoided by taking a few simple precautions around the house. If your baby does get burned, first check the wound to determine its severity. Then call the doctor. Do not try to treat anything more severe than a mild sunburn without consulting the pediatrician first.

DO

■ Hold the burned area under cold running water for at least 5 minutes, or until the pain subsides.

■ Immerse it in cold water (in a sink or bathtub) or use cold compresses if the burn is difficult to reach with a faucet.

■ Cover the burn with a sterile gauze bandage to reduce pain and protect any blisters.

■ Wrap the gauze loosely to avoid putting pressure on the burn.

DON'T

■ Put ice on the burn.

■ Use fluffy cotton, which may irritate the skin.

■ Give your child aspirin.

Insect Stings

If you're already aware that your baby has an insect allergy, seek emergency medical attention. If your pediatrician has prescribed an auto-injector of epinephrine, follow the instructions and administer it immediately. If there are no signs of circulation (breathing, coughing, or movement), begin CPR.

Mild reactions

SYMPTOMS: Swelling and mild pain

1 Brush off the stinger with a straight-edged object such as a credit card, or with your nail. Don't try to pull out the stinger—it might release more venom.

2 Wash the affected area with soap and water.

3 Apply a cold pack or cloth filled with ice.

4 Give your child an antihistamine containing diphenhydramine, such as Benadryl.

5 Apply hydrocortisone cream, calamine lotion, or a baking soda paste—with a ratio of 3 teaspoons baking soda to 1 teaspoon water—to the bite or sting several times a day until symptoms subside.

Contact your pediatrician immediately if:

- Swelling grows larger than 2 inches (5 cm).
- Swelling spreads, redness worsens, or fever develops.
- Child experiences stomach pain or has diarrhea.

Treating severe or allergic reactions step-by-step

SYMPTOMS: **Difficulty breathing, swelling lips or throat, faintness, dizziness, confusion, rapid heartbeat, nausea, hives, cramps, vomiting, or bleeding from the mouth**

1 Get immediate emergency medical attention.

2 If there are no signs of circulation, begin CPR. (See pages 121–124 for instructions.)

Animal or Human Bites

If your child's been bitten, first tend to the bite as you would any other wound. Then, you must identify what or who the culprit is and proceed accordingly.

If you know the animal's owner, contact that person and ask whether the animal is currently vaccinated against rabies. Even if the animal has been vaccinated, it should be observed and quarantined by a veterinarian for the next 10 days to see if it develops symptoms of rabies.

If the animal's history isn't known, contact the local health department. It will be assumed that the animal has rabies and you should start receiving treatment for rabies within 48 hours. If the animal is caught, it should be euthanised to test for rabies. Only if the test is negative can treatment be stopped.

Barely broken skin

1 Treat it as a minor wound.
2 Scrub the bite thoroughly with soap and running water.
3 Apply antibiotic cream and a loose sterile bandage.

Deep puncture or tear

1 Allow for some bleeding to cleanse the wound.
2 See your doctor immediately.

On the face, hand, foot, neck, over a joint

See your doctor immediately.

Choking

If you think your child might be choking, first note whether she's able to cough, gag, or talk. If she's coughing, let her continue to dislodge any blockages. If not, or if this doesn't work, follow the instructions below and seek emergency medical attention immediately.

For an Infant Back Blows and Chest Thrusts

▪ Position the face down on your forearm with your hand supporting the head and neck. Rest the arm holding your baby on your thigh.

▪ Support your baby so that the head is lower than the rest of the body. Then, using the heel of your hand, give 5 firm and distinct back blows between the shoulder blades to try to dislodge the object.

▪ Next, place your free hand (the one that had been delivering the back blows) on the back of your baby's head with your arm along the spine. Carefully turn your baby over while supporting the head and neck. Support your baby face up with your forearm resting on your thigh, still keeping the head lower than the rest of the body.

▪ Place the pads of 2 or 3 fingers just below an imaginary line running between your baby's nipples. To give a chest thrust, push straight down on the chest ½ to 1 inch (1 to 3 cm), then allow the chest to come back to its normal position.

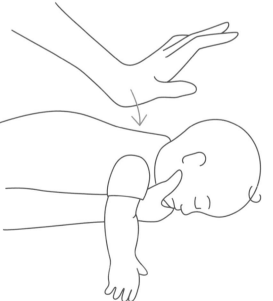

▪ Give 5 chest thrusts. The chest thrusts should be smooth, not jerky.

▪ Continue the sequence of 5 back blows and 5 chest thrusts until the object is forced out or your baby starts to cough. Let your child try to cough up the object.

▪ If your baby becomes unconscious at any time, you'll need to administer CPR (see full instructions starting on page 121).

For a Toddler Back Blows and Abdominal Thrusts

Stand or kneel behind your child. Provide support by placing one arm diagonally across the chest, and lean him or her forward.

Firmly strike your child between the shoulder blades with the heel of your other hand. Give 5 of these back blows.

Then wrap your arms around your child's waist. Make a fist with 1 hand and place the thumb side against the middle of your child's abdomen, just above the navel and well below the lower tip of the breastbone.

Grab your fist with your other hand and give 5 quick, inward thrusts into the abdomen. (Each back blow and abdominal thrust should be a separate and distinct attempt to dislodge the obstruction.)

Continue alternating 5 back blows and 5 abdominal thrusts until the object is dislodged or your child can breathe or cough forcefully.

If your child becomes unconscious, you'll need to administer CPR (see full instructions starting on page 121).

Falls

If your toddler takes a header, remember that if he's screaming, he's probably okay. Console your child and try to calm him down. Then check his limbs, head, and body for any bumps, bruises, cuts, redness, swelling, or deformity. If a bruise is painful to the touch, you can give him acetaminophen or ibuprofen. If your child is unconscious, but breathing, lay him on a flat surface and call emergency medical services. If he's not breathing, administer CPR. If you suspect a neck injury, don't move the child until a paramedic arrives.

Mild swelling

Apply ice pack to the injured or swollen area.

Bump or cut on the head

1 Apply ice pack to the injured or swollen area.

2 Observe child's mental state and behavior for any abrupt or worrying changes.

3 Call the doctor if you feel worried.

Minor cuts and scrapes

1 Clean with soap and water (harsher agents such as alcohol or hydrogen peroxide may actually damage tissue).

2 Apply an antibacterial cream or ointment.

3 Cover with a bandage.

Bleeding cuts

1 Apply firm pressure with clean gauze pad, towel, or cloth for 2 minutes or until bleeding decreases significantly or stops.

2 Elevate bleeding part above the heart.

3 Once bleeding slows or stops, clean wound and follow advice for minor cuts and scrapes. If bleeding does not stop, call doctor.

HOW TO USE AN ICE PACK

o You can use a commercial cold pack, crushed ice in a bag, or even a package of frozen vegetables.

o Never apply the ice pack directly to the skin; wrap in a towel or cloth first.

o Place the ice pack on the area of swelling; hold it gently but firmly for 20 minutes. Take a 5-minute break, then reapply for 20 minutes more.

112

Appendix

Appendix

Choosing a Pediatrician

The best way to find the right pediatrician: Ask your OB/gyn, friends, and neighbors for recommendations, and why they like a particular doctor. Choose a few pediatricians to interview, and bring a copy of this worksheet along on your visit so you will know what to look for and can rate your experience.

Pediatrician's name

Address   Phone numbers

Referred by   Insurance accepted

Hours   How to reach the practice after hours

Emergency policy   Group or solo practice

If group, what is the policy on seeing one or multiple docs?

Hospital affiliation   Web site/Do they e-mail with parents?

FIND OUT THE PEDIATRICIAN'S VIEWS ON

Bottle/Breastfeeding

Circumcision

Immunization

Sleeping, co-sleeping, sleep training

Other issues of importance to you

RATE THE OFFICE (SCALE OF 1 TO 4)

Cleanliness   Waiting room comfort (toys, seating, noise)   Typical waiting time

Separate waiting room for sick kids   Courteous, helpful staff   Convenience

OTHER NOTES

Selecting a Babysitter

Just when you've learned how to look after your baby, you face the somewhat daunting prospect of hiring someone else to do it. Whether the babysitter will be with your child for an hour or on a daily basis, you'll want to be certain you've chosen the right person for the job. Interview potential babysitters at your home and, if possible, with your baby present so they can interact. Make sure you call to check all references. Make copies of this worksheet and use it for your research.

Babysitter's name

Address

Home phone   Cell phone

Citizenship   Age

Does the potential sitter have children? How many and how old?

REFERENCES

Name   Phone

Comments

Name   Phone

Comments

Name   Phone

Comments

QUESTIONS TO ASK

Does the sitter have CPR and first aid certification?   Is he/she willing to obtain it?

What was his/her previous job(s)?

How did it end?

Ages of previous charges?

What does the sitter like about this job?

What activities does he/she like to do with children?

What is the babysitter's opinion on… (napping, television, discipline, toilet training, etc.)

Has he/she ever been in an emergency situation with a child? What happened?

Other subjects you may to want to ask about: Will the babysitter make meals, do laundry or other light housekeeping tasks, and take the child to activities? Can the sitter drive? Swim?

Does the sitter have questions for you?

OTHER NOTES

Choosing a Daycare Program

When looking for the right daycare program for your child, visit as many operations as you can, and talk to other parents about their experiences at each place. If your family lives in a major urban center, you may need to start looking at least 3 to 6 months before you anticipate needing daycare. Be prepared to sit on a waiting list. Make copies of this worksheet and use it for your research.

Name

Address

Phone

Owner/director   Cell phone

Hours of operation

Ratio of adult caregivers to children (should be at least 1 adult for every 3 to 4 infants, and 1 adult for every 4 to 6 children under the age of 3):

Staff training requirements

REFERENCES

Name   Phone

Name   Phone

RATE THE FACILITIES (SCALE OF 1 TO 4)

Cleanliness   Cheerfulness

Toys and play areas   Napping space

Changing areas/bathrooms   Secure outdoor space

Other impressions

Do children seem happy?

Do caregivers seem competent, content, affectionate, and responsive?

What safety precautions are in place? (First aid, childproofing, security, fire/smoke alarms, evacuation plan, food, cleanliness and handwashing policy, full background checks on staff members, supervision of children at all times, etc.)

What is the typical daily schedule?

What is the diaper changing routine?

What is the sick child policy?

Have there ever been any complaints lodged against this facility or its workers?

What is the annual staff turnover rate?

How are special needs recognized and accommodated?

What is the menu and how is food prepared?

What is the disciplinary policy?

How is children's development monitored?

What involvement do parents have?

My Baby's Data

Copy this sheet or use it as a model to create your own—one for every child. Post a copy near the phone or keep it with your important personal papers and make sure your children's caregivers know where to find it.

PERSONAL INFORMATION

Name

Date of birth	Birthplace (City, State)
Race	Color of skin

Hair color	Eye color	Blood type

Social security #	Identifying features/marks

CONTACT INFORMATION

Home address

Home phone number

Parent #1 name

Home phone	Cell phone

Home address (if different from above)

Work address	Work phone

Parent #2 name

Home phone	Cell phone

Home address (if different from above)

Work address	Work phone

Step-parent or other legal guardian name

Home phone   Cell phone

Home address (if different from above)

Work address   Work phone

Caregiver name

Home phone   Cell phone

Address

Emergency contact name

Home phone   Cell phone

Address

Nearest relative

Home phone   Cell phone

Address

Siblings (name/age)

DAYCARE/SCHOOL INFORMATION

Name

Address

Phone number

Director's name/number

Caregiver/teacher #1

Caregiver/teacher #2

Who is allowed to pick up child/relationship?

MEDICAL INFORMATION

Pediatrician name

Office phone   After hours phone

Address

Specialist name

Office phone   After hours phone

Address

Pharmacy name   Phone

Address

Hospital   Phone

Address

Emergency number (other than 911)

Poison control phone   Ambulance phone

ALLERGIES/SENSITIVITIES

CHRONIC MEDICAL CONDITIONS

Description

Treatment

Physician

REGULAR OR DAILY MEDICATIONS

Drug name   Dosage

Start/stop dates   What it does

Prescribed by

Vitamins or supplements

CPR, or cardiopulmonary resuscitation, is an essential emergency life-saving technique that all parents should know—whether your child is a newborn, kindergartner, or preteen. The following CPR instructions are not a substitute for CPR training. American Red Cross first-aid, CPR, and AED (automated external defibrillator) training can give you the skills and confidence to act in an emergency. Contact your local chapter or go to www.redcross.org for training information. Visit www.redcross.org/beredcrossready for CPR and first-aid online demonstrations.

Source: Information provided courtesy of The American Red Cross

CPR for Infants

1 ASSESS YOUR INFANT'S CONDITION.

- Check the scene for safety; check the baby.
- Flick your baby's foot or tap his shoulder and shout, "Are you okay?" to try to get his attention. If he's unresponsive, have someone call 9-1-1 or your local emergency number. If alone, give about 2 minutes of care, then call 9-1-1.
- On a hard, firm surface, lay your baby down on his back.
- Check for signs of life.

2 CHECK FOR SIGNS OF LIFE.

- With one hand on his forehead, tilt your baby's head back slightly, and with your other hand, lift his chin.
- Place your ear near your baby's mouth to check for signs of life (movement and breathing). Look at the chest, listen and feel for signs of breathing for no more than 10 seconds.
- If there are no signs of life, check the airway.

3 GIVE RESCUE BREATHS.

- Take a breath, making a complete seal with your mouth over the baby's mouth and nose.
- Give 2 rescue breaths. Breathe into the infant only until you see the chest clearly rise. Each breath should last 1 second.
- Pause between rescue breaths to let the air flow back out. Watch the chest clearly rise each time you breathe in to make sure that your rescue breaths are going in.
- If you notice NO movement in his chest, his airway is blocked. A blocked airway requires first aid for choking. See instructions in Chart 6.5, page 110.
- If the air goes in (chest clearly rises) check for severe bleeding and a pulse.
- To feel for your baby's pulse, place the pads of your index and middle fingers against the bone on the inside of your baby's upper arm between the elbow and the shoulder. Feel for a maximum of 10 seconds.

- If there are signs of life, but the infant is not breathing, give 1 rescue breath about every 3 seconds. After 2 minutes of rescue breathing, recheck the infant for breathing and other signs of life for no more than 10 seconds. If needed, continue until the scene becomes unsafe, he begins breathing on his own, you are too exhausted to continue or another trained responder takes over for you.

- If you do NOT feel a pulse, proceed with CPR.

4 ADMINISTER CPR.

- Place the pads of 2 or 3 fingers below an imaginary line running across the chest between the nipples, on the middle of the chest.

- Use the pads of these fingers to compress the chest. In a smooth motion, press straight down on his chest ½ to 1 inch (about 2 cm).

- Repeat compressions, performing 30 compressions in about 18 seconds (100 compressions per minute).

- After giving 30 compressions, give 2 rescue breaths as instructed in step 3.

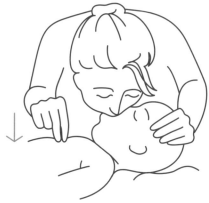

5 REPEAT CPR CYCLE.

- Continue the rounds of 30 chest compressions and 2 rescue breaths.

- If he revives, cease CPR and seek medical attention immediately.

- If he does not revive, continue CPR until the scene becomes unsafe, the infant shows signs of life, another trained responder arrives and takes over, or you are too exhausted to continue.

CPR for Toddlers

1 ASSESS YOUR TODDLER'S CONDITION.

- Check the scene for safety; check the toddler.

- Tap your toddler's shoulder and shout, "Are you okay?" to try to get his attention. If he's unresponsive, have someone call 9-1-1 or the local emergency number. Send someone to get an AED (automated external defibrillator), if available. If alone, give about 2 minutes of care, then call 9-1-1.

- On a hard, firm surface, lay your toddler down on his back.

- Check for signs of life.

2 CHECK FOR SIGNS OF LIFE.

- With one hand on his forehead, tilt your toddler's head back slightly, and with your other hand, lift his chin.

- Place your ear near your toddler's mouth to check for signs of life (movement and breathing). Look at the chest, listen and feel for signs of breathing for no more than 10 seconds.

- If there are no signs of life, check the airway

3 GIVE RESCUE BREATHS.

- Pinch your toddler's nostrils shut and, after taking a breath, make a complete seal around his mouth with your mouth.

- Breathe into the toddler until you see the chest clearly rise. Pause between rescue breaths to let the air flow out. Watch the toddler's chest clearly rise each time you breathe in to make sure that your rescue breaths are going in.

- If you notice NO movement in his chest, his airway is blocked. A blocked airway requires first aid for choking. See instructions in Chart 6.5, page 111.

- If the air goes in (chest clearly rises) check for severe bleeding and a pulse.

- To feel for your toddler's pulse, place the pads of your index and middle fingers on the center of his throat, and slide them into the groove at the side of the neck. Feel for a maximum of 10 seconds.

- If there are signs of life, but the toddler is not breathing, give 1 rescue breath about every 3 seconds. After 2 minutes of rescue breathing, recheck the toddler for breathing and other signs of life for no more than 10 seconds. If needed, continue until the scene becomes unsafe, he begins breathing on his own, you are too exhausted to continue, or another trained responder takes over for you.

- If you do NOT feel a pulse, proceed with CPR.

4 ADMINISTER CPR.

- Find the center of your toddler's chest, and place the base of 1 palm on his breastbone, or sternum.

- Place your other hand directly on top of the first hand and try to keep your fingers off the chest by interlacing them or holding them upward. Alternatively, you can use a one-handed technique by placing one hand on the toddler's chest and the other hand on the forehead to maintain an open airway.

- Position your body correctly by kneeling beside the toddler, placing your hands in the correct position, straightening your arms and locking your elbows so that your shoulders are directly over your hands.

- Compress the chest smoothly to a depth of about 1½ inches (about 4 cm) using the heel of the dominant hand.

- After each compression, wait until his chest rises before compressing again.

- Repeat compressions, performing 30 compressions in about 18 seconds (100 compressions per minute).

- After giving 30 compressions, remove your compression hand(s) from the chest, tilt his head back and give 2 rescue breaths, as instructed in step 3. After giving the breaths, place your hand(s) in the same position as before and continue compressions.

5 REPEAT CPR CYCLE.

- Continue the rounds of 30 chest compressions and 2 rescue breaths.

- If he revives, cease CPR and seek medical attention immediately.

- If he does not revive, continue CPR until the scene becomes unsafe, the toddler shows signs of life, an AED becomes available and is ready to use, another trained responder arrives and takes over, or you are too exhausted to continue.

Resources for Parents

American Academy of Allergy Asthma & Immunology
555 East Wells Street
Suite 1100
Milwaukee, WI 53202-3823
Phone: 414-272-6071
E-mail: info@aaaai.org
Web site: www.aaaai.org

American Academy of Pediatrics
141 Northwest Point Boulevard
PO Box 747
Elk Grove Village, IL 60009-0747
Phone: 1-888-227-1770
  Fax: 847-228-1281
E-mail: kidsdocs@aap.org
Web site: www.aap.org

American Association of Poison Control Centers
3201 New Mexico Avenue, Suite 330
Washington, DC 20016
Phone: 202-362-7217
  Emergency Phone: 1-800-222-1222
Email: info@aapcc.org
Web site: www.aapcc.org

American Red Cross
National Headquarters
2025 E Street, NW
Washington, DC 20006
Phone: 703-206-6000
Web site: www.redcross.org

Centers for Disease Control and Prevention
1600 Clifton Road
Atlanta, GA 30333
Phone: 404-498-1515
  Toll Free Phone: 1-800-311-3435
Web site: www.cdc.gov

Kids with Food Allergies
73 Old Dublin Pike
  Suite 10, #163
Doylestown, PA 18901
Phone: 215-230-5394
  Fax: 215-340-7674
Web site:
  www.kidswithfoodallergies.org

National Child Care Information and Technical Assistance Center
10530 Rosehaven Street, Suite 400
Fairfax, VA 22030
Phone: 1-800-616-2242
  Fax: 1-800-716-2242
E-mail: info@nccic.org
Web site: nccic.org

National Healthy Start Association
1220 19th Street, NW, Suite 801
Washington, DC 20036-2435
Phone: 202-296-2195
  Fax: 202-296-2197
E-mail:
  kduncan@nationalhealthystart.org
Web site:
  www.healthystartassoc.org

National Resource Center for Health and Safety in Child Care and Early Education
UCD-SON Campus Mail Stop F541
Education 2 North
13120 E. 19th Avenue
Aurora, CO 80045-0508
Phone: 1-800-598-KIDS
  Fax: 303-724-0960
E-mail: natl.child.res.ctr@uchsc.edu
Web site: nrc.uchsc.edu

National Safety Council
1121 Spring Lake Drive
Itasca, IL 60143-3201
Phone: 630-285-1121
  Fax: 630-285-1315
Web site: www.nsc.org

National Sudden Infant Death Resource Center
2115 Wisconsin Avenue, NW,
  Suite 601
Washington, DC 20007-2292
Phone: 202-687-7466
  Toll Free Phone: 1-866-866-7437
Fax: 202-784-9777
E-mail: info@sidscenter.org
Web site: www.sidscenter.org

US Consumer Product Safety Commission
4330 East West Highway
Bethesda, MD 20814
Toll Free Hotline: 1-800-638-2772
  (hours: 8:30 am to 5 pm EST)
Phone: 301-504-7923
  Fax: 301-504-0124 &
  301-504-0025
Web site: www.cpsc.gov

Zero to Three: National Center for Infants, Toddlers and Families
2000 M Street, NW, Suite 200
Washington, DC 20036
Phone: 202-638-1144
  Fax: 202-638-0851
Web site: www.zerotothree.org

ONLINE RESOURCES

American Baby, Family Circle, Parents online magazines
www.parents.com

Baby Center
www.babycenter.com

The Dr. Spock Company
www.drspock.com

Home & Family Network
www.homeandfamilynetwork.com

Keep Kids Healthy
www.keepkidshealthy.com

Nemours Foundation's Center for Children's Health Media
www.kidshealth.org

Nutrition Explorations
www.nutritionexplorations.org

FURTHER READING

American Academy of Pediatrics. *Caring For Your Baby and Young Child: Birth to Age Five*. New York: Bantam Books, 1998.

Leach, Penelope. *Your Baby & Child: From Birth to Age Five*. New York: Knopf, 1997.

Sears, William, MD, Martha Sears, R.N., Robert Sears, MD, and James Sears, MD. *The Baby Book: Everything You Need to Know About Your Baby From Birth to Age Two*. New York: Little, Brown and Company, 2003.

Spock, Benjamin, MD. *Dr. Spock's Baby and Child Care*. New York: Simon & Schuster, 2004.

Index

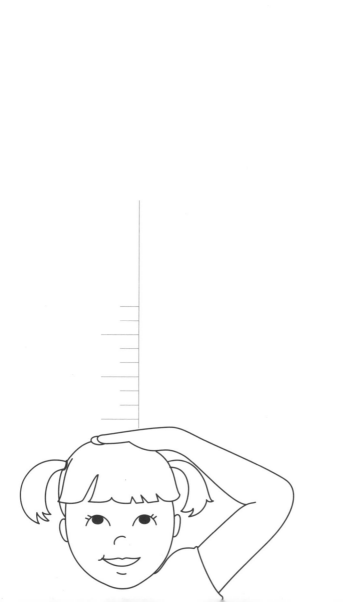